The Compassionate Geek

Mastering Customer Service for IT Professionals

Second Edition
Revision 2.1

Don R. Crawley, Linux+, CCNA Security
Paul R. Senness, MBA

Seattle, Washington

www.soundtraining.net

Reasonable attempts have been made to ensure the accuracy of the information contained in this publication as of the date on which it was written. This publication is distributed in the hope that it will be helpful, but with no guarantees. There are no guarantees made as to the accuracy, reliability, or applicability of this information for any task or purpose whatsoever.

The authors recommend that these techniques be used only as a guide to working with end users. Under no circumstances should these techniques be considered universal rules for working with all people in all situations.

ISBN-13: 978-0-9836-6070-5

For libraries and academic institutions: ISBN: 978-1-4537-1278-8

PO Box 48094
Seattle, Washington 98148-0094
United States of America
On the web: www.soundtraining.net
On the phone: (206) 988-5858
Email: info@soundtraining.net

com·pas·sion (kəm-'păsh-ən), *n.,* Profound awareness of another's suffering combined with the desire to alleviate it.

geek (gēk), *slang, n.,* A term of pride referring to a computer expert

About soundtraining.net...

soundtraining.net is a Seattle-based company that provides advanced technical training in an accelerated one- and two-day format to IT professionals. soundtraining.net's students include network administrators, network engineers, support desk personnel, and anyone involved in computer network design, installation, operation, and maintenance. soundtraining.net specializes in Cisco and Linux product training, plus workplace skills training for IT professionals.

Among the training topics offered by soundtraining.net are:

- Cisco ASA Security Appliance Training: Installing, Configuring, Optimizing, and Troubleshooting
- Cisco Router Fundamentals 2-Day Hands On Workshop
- Networking Fundamentals
- Linux Server Training: Installing, Configuring, Optimizing, and Troubleshooting
- How to Deliver Outstanding Customer Service
- Project Management for IT Professionals Two Day Seminar
- Secrets of Successful Time and Task Management Using Outlook
- Managing and Supervising People for Positive Results

Subscribe to our newsletter for the latest information about new classes, blog posts, and special offers: **www.soundtraining.net/newsletter**

soundtraining.net can present training onsite, at your location, at your convenience. Call **(206) 988-5858** or email **onsite@soundtraining.net**.

soundtraining.net
accelerated i.t. training

PO Box 48094
Seattle, WA 98148-0094
www.soundtraining.net

Contents

"Technology, like art, is a soaring exercise of the human imagination."

—Daniel Bell, The Winding Passage, 1980

Introduction

Those of us who are IT support staff have, as a fundamental part of our jobs, helping our end users work more productively, efficiently, and creatively. Our jobs are not so much about technology as about delivering creative solutions to workplace problems. Technology is merely the vehicle we use to get the job done.

For that reason, outstanding end-user support is not just a matter of having great technical knowledge. The great desktop support technicians build great IT careers by also understanding the importance of human-relations. Part technologist, part psychologist, the exceptional desktop support staffer understands that there is an art to using technology as the solution for workplace problems. This book will focus on helping the IT professional deliver great end-user support by knowing how to combine the technical aspects of the job with an empathetic (and occasionally sympathetic) ear.

Many technical support positions have been outsourced in recent years. The IT support staffer who understands that the job is as much about "human relations" skills as technical skills is becoming increasingly more valuable as organizations become more dependent upon technology and the people who support it. This book will help you win advocates among your users. Advocates will speak up for you behind your back, at the water cooler or the coffee machine. The more advocates you have, the more secure your job will be and you'll have more career opportunities, both in your current company and in other firms as your users take new positions within and outside the existing company.

Congratulations! The fact that you're reading this book puts you ahead of the game, because it means that you understand the importance of the human element of IT.

Acknowledgements

This book began life as a seminar workbook when Ted Loran at the State of Washington asked my company to develop a customer service workshop for IT staff. One thing led to another and now it has grown into a full-fledged book!

Thanks to Janet, my wife, and the rest of my family, to my longtime friend and partner on this book, Paul Senness, for his writing, counsel, and friendship, to Cleo the dog for being such a great teacher and companion, to Kathy Gangwisch of Gangwisch and Associates, to Mark Morgan who introduced me to key people at the State of Washington, to Ted Loran at the State of Washington, to Stacey Barker at Discover Financial, to Erik Seastedt at SUNY Cobleskill, to Navid Mansourian at Facebook, to Michael Natale at LogMeIn, and all of the IT folks who understand the importance of the delighted user.
--Don R. Crawley, http://www.doncrawley.com

I am indebted to Don Crawley for giving me the opportunity to help write this book. It was a huge undertaking putting my part together, which he told me up front it would be. I gained a real appreciation for the extraordinary efforts he has made in producing his other books and I'm grateful for his confidence and encouragement throughout this project. Also, thanks to Janet Crawley for her infectious optimism and positive outlook at life. I am indeed fortunate to have the friendship of these two incredible people. Finally, thanks to the literally thousands of people I've come in contact with through my speaking career. I have learned much from your experiences and insights about what it means to really take care of people.
--Paul R. Senness, http://paulsenness.smugmug.com

Online Resources and Social Networking

There are two collections of online videos to supplement the information in this book. You'll find them at www.doncrawley.com/videos and at www.soundtraining.net/videos

Don blogs on customer service and communication at www.compassionategeek.com. He also blogs on technical issues at www.soundtraining.net/blog.

He also maintains a Facebook page at www.doncrawley.com/fb, tweets at www.doncrawley.com/twitter, and you can connect with him on LinkedIn at www.doncrawley.com/linkedin

Announcements about new books, videos, and other resources are made through major social networking channels and to the newsletter mailing list. You can subscribe at www.doncrawley.com/newsletter.

Although it's not related to customer service, you might enjoy seeing Paul's award-winning underwater photography at http://paulsenness.smugmug.com

12

Chapter One:
The Foundations of Service

"People will forget what you say, they will forget what you do, but they never will forget how you make them feel."

--Dr. Maya Angelou

Interactive Exercise: Remembering the Good, the Bad, and the Awful

This exercise is designed to help you recall both good and bad technical support situations in which you were the one receiving technical support. In the column labeled "Heroes", write two or three incidents in which you felt you received excellent technical support. In the column labeled "Villains", write down two or three incidents in which you felt you received really bad technical support. (You might want to use a separate sheet of paper for this exercise. You'll be referring to it later in the book.)

Heroes	*Villains*

Now, take a moment and write down in each of the following columns the things that were happening during the technical support session that make it good or bad. Write down the good things in the "Hero Behaviors" column and write down the bad things in the "Villain Behaviors" column:

Hero Behaviors	Villain Behaviors

As you read through the rest of the book, reflect back on the two preceding tables. Think about what makes a great support session, what makes a poor support session, and about your own experiences, both good and bad, providing support as an IT support professional.

Is it something intrinsic?

Great customer service is about your user's experience. Your competitors sell products and services that are quite similar, if not identical, to yours; they may even be priced similarly to yours. What makes a difference to your users is their experience; how you make them feel.

Everybody talks about customer service, lots of people teach customer service, but I began to wonder if there might be some foundational, or **intrinsic**, skills that could guide you in serving your user. As a trainer and consultant working with organizations and industries as diverse as Facebook, state government, healthcare, universities, and financial services, I observed that within every organization, there are usually key individuals who simply "get it". When given a choice, users always go back to them, not only when they have problems, but for every type of interaction with the organization. As we observed those individuals in our workshops, we began to see common traits emerge. In fact, it seems that there are really four traits, intrinsic qualities, that are common to the individuals who, even without training, simply seem to know how to deal effectively with their users.

Bonus Video: Watch a video about the Four Traits of the Customer Service Masters at www.doncrawley.com/videos

Empathy

"Taught by time, my heart has learned to glow for other's good, and melt at other's woe."
--Homer

The first of those traits is **empathy**. Empathy is the ability to connect with another individual emotionally; to feel what they're feeling. It's often known as "putting yourself in someone else's shoes" or "walking a mile in another's shoes". In our customer service workshops, we recommend the use of empathetic phrases such as "I'd feel that way, too, if it happened to me.", "I don't blame you for feeling that way. I'd be as upset as you are in your position.", or "I can see how frustrated you are and I don't blame you." It's also important to be authentic...sincere...in your empathy. If you simply can't relate to your user's situation, it's okay to say so when you combine it with human understanding. For example, you can say things like, "I've never been in your situation, so I'm not going to tell you I understand. I can't even imagine what that's like, but I am going to do everything within my power to help you. I'm sure if I were in your situation, I'd feel the same way you do." The key is sincere, human-to-human empathy.

Compassion

"Compassion is the antitoxin of the soul: where there is compassion even the most poisonous impulses remain relatively harmless."
--Eric Hoffer

The second trait is very much related to the first and it is **compassion**. Compassion is the act of caring about the well-being of another. It really boils down to the timeless wisdom of the Golden Rule: Treat others the way you would have them treat you.

Another way to think of compassion in customer service is, "Doing it with heart".

Like empathy, compassion is about one human relating to another human. When our users place themselves in our care, they are first and foremost a human being. We may not like their political views, we may not like the way they look or act. Frankly, we may not like anything about them, but they are still human beings deserving of our human-to-human care, understanding, and respect.

When you genuinely care about what happens to other people, you instinctively look for ways to better their experience.

"We teach our children that everyone is entitled to dignity and respect." --David E. Kelly

Listening

"To be able to listen to others in a sympathetic and understanding manner is perhaps the most effective mechanism in the world for getting along with people and tying up their friendship for good."

"It is the province of knowledge to speak and it is the privilege of wisdom to listen."
--Oliver Wendell Holmes

The third trait is the ability to **listen**. This means that your sole focus is on what your user is saying.

There are three steps to effective listening:

1. Hearing. Hearing means that you're listening enough to know what the speaker is saying.
2. Understanding. Understanding means you relate what you've heard to your own experiences and knowledge.
3. Processing. Processing is the act of taking what you understood the speaker to say and evaluating it.

Effective listening is enhanced by a "human moment" in which you are attuned to the other person. According to psychiatrist Dr. Edward M. Hallowell, "To make the human moment work, you have to set aside what you're doing, put down the memo you were reading, disengage from your laptop, abandon your daydream, and focus on the person you're with. Usually when you do that, the other person will feel the energy and respond in kind."

A technique that can help you become a better listener is to listen as though you're going to be tested on what is being said. If you know there's a quiz coming up, you'll find a way to sharpen your focus on the speaker. Author and speaker Stephen Covey recommends repeating back what is said, using phrases such as, "Let me make sure I understand. The problem is…"

Respect

"Respect for ourselves guides our morals, respect for others guides our manners."
--Laurence Sterne

"Respect a man, he will do the more."
--James Howell

The fourth essential skill is the ability to treat all people with **respect**, regardless of how you might feel about them. In fact, it's not necessary to respect someone to treat him or her with respect. Respecting someone is a matter of how you feel about that person and whether they have earned your respect. Treating someone with respect is a matter of your behavior and, frankly, is a reflection of how you feel about yourself. Certainly, people must earn our respect; regardless of whether someone has earned our respect, all people should be treated with respect and dignity. It is a matter of your own dignity and character that you treat all things respectfully.

In the movie *The Green Mile*, Tom Hanks' character was a death-row prison guard. He was charged with guarding condemned convicts who had performed some terrible crimes. You could certainly argue that the men in his care were not deserving of respect, yet he treated them all respectfully. It may have been the first and only time in their lives when any of them were treated respectfully.

We must also respect ourselves. We respect ourselves when we accept full responsibility for ourselves. We may not be in complete control of the things that happen to us, but we are in complete control of how we respond to those things. Examples of how we respect ourselves might include making respectful choices in the foods we eat, drinking water every day, avoiding destructive behaviors, and choosing friends and colleagues who are positive, up-lifting influences in our lives.

In our role as a provider of service to people, we may find ourselves dealing with people we don't like or respect. We maintain our own dignity and self-respect when we treat all living things respectfully. In his landmark book, *Man's Search for Meaning*, author Viktor Frankl suggests that the true measure of an individual lies not in his or her usefulness, but in his or her ability to maintain a sense of dignity in all circumstances. It's easy to be arrogant and judgmental; it's more difficult and infinitely more meaningful to maintain your dignity in the face of undignified situations and people.

Chapter Two:
The Challenge of Different Generations

"Blessed is the
generation in which the
old listen to the young;
and doubly blessed is
the generation in which
the young listen to the
old"

–Talmud

Today's workplace has greater diversity among its employees than at any other time in our history. Just recently, it seemed as though we managed a fairly homogeneous group of people, meaning they were all about the same age and sex with similar racial/ethnic backgrounds and they all came from equally similar socio/cultural environments. It required only a few tools and just a moderate understanding of these issues to manage a workforce. But today the situation is radically changed: The workgroup you manage is very likely composed of men and women of all age groups with differing racial/ethnic backgrounds as well as widely ranging socio/economic backgrounds. Much has been written about these differences in all areas except age. Generational differences are often the least understood of these topics. In this chapter you will examine the way people of different age groups look at the world, the workplace, and technology.

- What are the four generational groups at work?
- How have world and national events shaped their view of the workplace?
- Where do the loyalties of each group lie?
- To which group do the IT managers belong?
- Who are the IT support professionals?
- What are the potential pitfalls dealing with each group?

Generations in the workplace

Researchers say that today there are four distinct generations in the US workplace, based on year of birth. Although there have always been different age groups working throughout our history, world events of the last century and the change from a largely agrarian society to one of technology has impacted the US work environment like no other in the world. As a result, four "work" generations have emerged, each with their own view towards the world, and especially the workplace. Understanding these differences can help IT managers and IT support professionals recognize potential areas of conflict and be better prepared to deal with them.

Historical Events and the Generations

To start our understating of the generations it is worth looking at historical events in a timeline. Our individual worldview is largely shaped by the environment in which we grew up and the lessons we learned from our parents, relatives, teachers, neighbors, and friends.

A successful radio station programming consultant observed that the popular music of your teenage and early post-teen years becomes "the music of your life". Similarly, the events taking place during our formative years can shape our view of our world, from our families to our communities to our nation and world.

Human-Beings are Unique

Like much research into human behavior, the descriptions of generational differences are stereotypes, and cannot and should not be applied with absolute certainty – but they are a good place to begin.

The table on the next page shows some of the major influencers by decade. What are some of the things you recall from your adolescent and teenage years? For example, members of the Veterans generation can tell you exactly where they were and what they were doing when the Japanese attacked Pearl Harbor. Baby-Boomers can tell you exactly where they were and what they were doing when President Kennedy was shot. Certainly, members of all generations recall where they were and what they were doing when the World Trade Center was attacked. The attack is a defining moment, however, for the Millennial generation. Identifying a defining moment for Gen Xers has been difficult for generational researchers. In a non-scientific study of several Gen Xers, individuals mentioned things such as the death of Lady Di or Kurt Cobain's suicide, but there was not general agreement on a single defining moment.

Decade	Significant Events
1930s	Stock Market Crash, Great Depression, Election of FDR
1940s	Pearl Harbor, Death of FDR, D-Day, First use of atomic weapons, end of World War II, start of the Cold War
1950s	McCarthy hearings, Korean War, television, Elvis Presley and the start of Rock 'n Roll, polio vaccine introduced, Brown vs. Board of Education
1960s	Vietnam, Kennedy elected, civil rights movement, Kennedy/King assassinations, space race and moon landing, Cold War intensification, Cuban missile crisis, Woodstock, the Beatles, birth control pill
1970s	Oil embargo, Watergate, Nixon resignation, appearance of PCs, Roe vs. Wade, women's rights, Iran hostage situation, rap/hip-hop music
1980s	Fall of Berlin Wall, Challenger disaster, John Lennon killed, Reagan elected, Iran contra scandal
1990s	Desert Storm, Oklahoma City bombing, Clinton scandals
2000s	World Trade Center attack, Election of President George W. Bush, Iraq war, Pope John Paul II dies, Election of President Barack Obama

By using the preceding table as we consider the generations in today's workforce, it is possible to identify some clues as to why they are the way they are. Different authors use slightly different years as divisional points. They are, for the most part, a matter of convenience for discussion, and in no case did the characteristics of the individual generations change overnight.

1922 – 1943: The Veterans

This group of workers has been referred to as the Veterans, GI Generation, Radio Generation, and the Silent Generation. They grew up coming out of the American economic depression and the recovery from World War II. Because they and their parents endured the hardships of much higher unemployment, they learned that getting and keeping a job required "doing what the boss said." Because the available labor pool was fairly large, a management technique that worked was "my way or the highway" which led to the moniker "silent generation." These workers knew not to rock the boat. As a group they are very steady and reliable workers. They show up for work early and go home late. Their loyalty is to the company, and it was not uncommon for them to be with the same firm their entire career. They learned to "work hard today for delayed reward tomorrow."

They have observed the pace of technology increase throughout their lives. As children, America was a strong mix of agrarian and industrial work environments. The type of labor required was primarily manual. As they progressed through their careers they saw technology change from requiring a few basic hand tools and a modicum of common sense to fix almost anything, to an era of specialized equipment and knowledge for almost every task. (Think about the changes in automobile maintenance during their lives!) They are not change-phobic, but they can be intimidated and confused by rapid change. They can and do want to use computers as a work tool, but require more time to learn programs. Because they are focused on getting things done they tend to be less interested in knowing multiple ways of accomplishing the same task. They tend to prefer a consistent environment.

1943 – 1960: Baby Boomers

Baby boomers grew up in the relative prosperity of an America transformed by the Veterans. They too learned from their parents what would be considered a strong work ethic, but also believed there was more to life than just work. They came of age in a world of improving communications and technology with the advent of television and electric everything. The early boomers were on the leading edge of the civil rights movement, and were significantly impacted by the Kennedy/King assassinations, Vietnam War, and Watergate/Nixon scandals. One result was that they coined the phrase "trust no one over thirty." In various degrees they became anti-establishment. One of the results of this is that their loyalty moved from the company to themselves. They are good team players, but in the end they are more interested in "what's in it for me."

Boomers tend to be work-aholics and play-aholics. They work hard, play hard and have lots of toys. They are always on the move with lives full of activity. They can easily burn themselves out. They can be motivated by power, position, and prestige. They saw the beginnings of and endured the downsizing of corporate America, losing their jobs for no other reason that being in the wrong place at the wrong time.

1960 – 1980: Generation X

One of the most studied generations in the workforce today is Generation X. As children of the late Veterans and the Boomers, they mark a significant change in attitude towards the workplace. They grew up in an era of increasing technology and became very adept with it. In fact, this is the generation in which we see a role reversal regarding technology. They understand and know more about its use than their parents.

As a group they tend to be independent, cynical, and highly mobile. For the most part they raised themselves as "latch key kids" since their parents both worked. They saw their parents lose their jobs for what seemed no logical reason and learned to not trust the company. Who they do trust are their friends and siblings, and that is where their loyalties lie – to those relationships. They have little interest in spending the bulk of their time in the workplace. In fact, they work to live and will job hop in order to achieve that end. They are quite resistant to "do it my way" or "we do it this way because the book says so." They want to understand the reasons why things are done the way they are.

They may build very close relationships with their co-workers and work place behaviors can include taking breaks together, "doing lunch" together, and socializing with each other in the evenings and on weekends. This tight bonding can and has led to the entire team quitting when only one of them is upset or perceives mistreatment by the organization. The lower unemployment is in a sector, or the higher the demand for a scarce technical skill-set, the higher the probability there is of this occurring.

1980 – Present: The Millennials (Generation Y or Nexters)

The final generation currently identified in today's workplace is Generation Y, sometimes referred to the Millennials, or the Nexters. It is unclear where their loyalties are going to lie, but there are some strong characteristics already visible. Like Gen X, they are resistant to "do it my way." They want and need to understand the "why" of things. Their moral values tend to mirror those of the Veterans who seem to be their heroes. They grew up with technology and are used to the fast pace it brings to all aspects of life. Much of their communications with others started with email, then instant messaging, and today it is texting. Some people say they are in to instantaneous gratification - the only problem is it takes too long! They almost demand change (which contrasts significantly with the Veterans).

It is very important to remember that these descriptions are stereotypes. Although peoples' characteristics trend into these categories, there are many exceptions. For example, employees who grew up in rural areas, and in particular on a farm or ranch, will have what many consider a strong work ethic regardless of year of birth. Those who grew up in major metropolitan areas seem to fall more strongly into the described categories, but here again there are exceptions. And finally, there is evidence that some people shift their workplace attitude as they age. As an example, some of the boomers are adopting attitudes more like those of Gen X.

Summarizing the Four Generations

	Veterans	*Boomers*	*Xers*	*Millennials*
Outlook	Practical	Optimistic	Skeptical	Hopeful
Work ethic	Dedicated	Driven	Balanced	Determined
View of authority	Respectful	Love/Hate	Unimpressed	Polite
Leadership by	Hierarchy	Consensus	Competence	Pulling together
Relationships	Personal sacrifice	Personal gratification	Reluctant to commit	Inclusive

Figure 1 From Generations at Work by Ron Zemke, Claire Raines, and Bob Filipczak © 2000

34

Communicating with the Generations

Regardless of the generation with whom you are communicating, there are three communication guidelines that are universal:

- Be respectful, never condescending.
- Keep it professional, avoid pet-phrases and slang (even when you know someone well, it is best to keep such language out of the workplace). Although this suggestion may seem stilted, there is no harm in maintaining a friendly, but professional demeanor in the workplace. There is, however, great potential for career harm in being perceived as too casual and unprofessional in the workplace.
- Don't take yourself too seriously.

Again, Human-Beings are Unique

As mentioned earlier, these are guidelines and certainly not hard and fast rules. First and foremost, remember that you are dealing with human beings, each of whom brings a unique set of experiences and expectations to his interaction with you. The following guidelines provide a starting point for choosing a communication style, based on generational memberships. You can also ask the individual how she would prefer you communicate with her.

Regardless, you'll rarely go wrong by maintaining an air of friendly and respectful professionalism.

Communicating with Veterans (Traditionalists)

- Use face-to-face or written communication.
- Members of this generation tend to be more private, don't expect them to immediately share their thoughts or feelings.

- They will tend to pay more attention to the words you say than to your gestures and other forms of body language. Choose your words wisely!

Communicating with Baby Boomers

- Show flexibility by presenting options.
- Be open and direct, but not controlling or manipulating.
- Give complete, thorough answers to questions and expect follow up questions.

Communicating with Generation Xers

- Use an informal communication style (while maintaining professionalism).
- Email should be your first choice for communication.
- Use short sound bites to communicate to keep their attention.
- Be inclusive; share information frequently.
- Be prepared to give and receive feedback.

Communicating with Millennials (Gen Yers)

- Use texting, IMing, or Facebook for communication.
- As with Gen Xers, be prepared to give and receive feedback regularly.
- Encourage them to try new things and find new ways of learning.

Chapter Three:
Practical Emotional Intelligence

"…respect, tolerance and understanding for culture and religion are absolutely necessary in times of challenge and controversy. They are, in fact, the roots of character in times of great stress…"

—Army Lt. Col. Christopher P. Hughes

Emotional Intelligence is a frequently-used term in today's business circles. It refers to your ability to identify your own emotions and the emotions of others and respond appropriately.

- The ability to recognize and respond to emotions in yourself and others
- The ability to respond appropriately to emotions
- The ability to control your own emotions
- The ability to influence a desired emotional response in others

Is the practice of emotional intelligence important and does it work? Consider the following story:

In April of 2003, Army Lt. Col. Christopher Hughes was leading a group of soldiers to meet with Ayatollah Sistani in the Iraqi city of An Najaf. They had been invited by the Ayatollah to discuss a fatwa, a religious proclamation, to help stop fighting in the city. As Hughes and his soldiers approached the mosque, an angry crowd of Iraqis confronted the patrol. Agitators had spread rumors that the soldiers were going to arrest the Ayatollah. As the crowd grew, becoming more agitated and aggressive, Col. Hughes initially thought to fire warning shots into the air, but he reconsidered and instead told his soldiers to "take a knee", point their weapons to the ground, and smile. The colonel recognized that the crowd didn't understand the patrol's intention and that he had to find a way to communicate to them that he and his soldiers were not a threat. Upon seeing the soldier's non-threatening stance and actions, the crowd's mood morphed from agitation to relief. Colonel Hughes then ordered the patrol to retreat and, as they retreated, he turned, faced the crowd, put his right-hand over his heart, and bowed, a gesture of respect that means "Allah be praised". The colonel could have taken a more traditional approach to conflict and fired his weapon, but by responding in an emotionally intelligent manner, he diffused an explosive situation. Not only were he and his soldiers able to retreat safely, they achieved a PR coup that undermined the agitators attempts to cast the Americans in a bad light. What's more, that night the Ayatollah issued a fatwa to the people of

Najaf telling them not to interfere with the Americans entering the city.[1]

Emotional Maturity

The study of Emotional Intelligence actually goes back to Darwin's early work studying the importance of emotional expression for survival. In the early 1900s, researchers coined the term "social intelligence" to describe the skill of understanding and managing other people.

Several researchers studied emotional intelligence throughout the 20th century, but the concept of emotional intelligence really took hold with the 1997 release of author and psychologist Daniel Goleman's best-selling book *Emotional Intelligence: Why it Can Matter more than IQ*. His 2006 book, *Social Intelligence: The New Science of Social Relationships*, continues his work on emotional intelligence, but also suggests that our brains are physically wired to connect with one another.

This chapter is based, to a great extent, on the work of Daniel Goleman.

According to Goleman, emotional intelligence is all about how we handle ourselves and how we handle relationships.

Emotional Intelligence is both an academic pursuit and a practical or lifestyle pursuit. This chapter is concerned with the practical aspects of emotional intelligence. There is a body of thought that suggests emotional intelligence is more important as a measure of ability than intellect.

---

[1] http://www.conscienceandcourage.org/volume4/Story5.php

From a practical standpoint, emotional intelligence involves three areas or abilities:

1. The ability to recognize and respond to emotions in yourself and others
2. The ability to control your own emotions
3. The ability to influence a desired emotional response in others

For the purpose of this chapter, it may help you to think of emotional intelligence as emotional maturity.

Gradually, as we live and experience different people and situations, we develop methods of responding to those people and situations. Sometimes, we learn how to deal with people and situations by watching others such as our parents, teachers, respected friends, or celebrities. Other times, we read and study how to react to various people and situations. Often, our responses are shaped by a combination of external influences and things we read and study.

The Ability to Recognize and Respond to Emotions in Yourself and Others

The ability to recognize emotions in others through facial expressions, tone-of-voice, verbal language, and body language is what allows you to move into the remaining abilities. Similarly, the ability to recognize emotions within yourself through feelings and physical responses also allows you to move into the remaining abilities.

Look at the faces in the pictures below. Can you tell what the people are thinking based on their expressions? Are you sure?

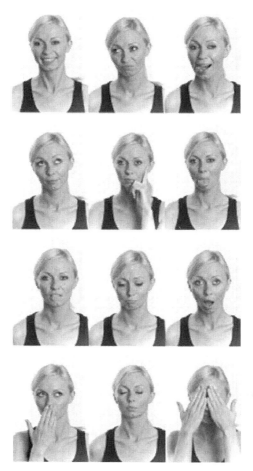

Figure 2 Examples of facial expressions

Figure 3 More examples of facial expressions

Sometimes, it's possible to tell how or what a person is feeling by his or her facial expressions. Other times, however, a deeper connection with the individual is required. According to Goleman, our brains are physically wired to connect with other people. Measurable changes in brain behavior occur when one individual connects with another. It's not limited just to humans; similar changes in brain activity occur in other animals. He calls this phenomenon the "social brain". Think about the times in your life when you've really connected with another person; perhaps at the start of a new friendship or romance, maybe in a really good job interview. What's really happening is that you and the other person are establishing rapport.

A State of Rapport

Goleman believes that there are three ingredients of rapport:

1. Both people are paying attention; you're really attuned to each other
2. The non-verbal communications such as your gestures and body language, look like a choreographed dance
3. It feels good.

The key for you, as a support person, starts with the first ingredient. You must pay careful attention to what your user is saying. In other parts of this workbook, we mention repeating back what the user says with phrases such as:

"Let me make sure I understand you correctly. Your printer is printing pages upside down. Is that correct?"

"Just to be sure I understand, let me repeat this back to you. You're able to connect to internal sites with no problem, but when you try to hit the Internet, you get a 404 error. Is that correct?"

Repeating back the issue(s) does three things: It helps ensure that you really do understand the issue. It helps the user feel comfortable that you really do understand the issue. It starts the process of establishing rapport with your user.

Researchers have discovered that the areas of our brain responsible for calming us under stress work more effectively in the presence of an empathetic person. As a tech support person, you are that empathetic person. Your calm, empathetic behavior actually triggers changes in the other person's brain chemistry helping them become more calm, even under stress.

In an article for the Harvard Business Review titled "The Human Moment", psychiatrist Edward M. Hallowell writes about how to make contact with other people at work. Hallowell suggests that in order to create a human moment in which you truly connect with your co-workers, two ingredients must exist:

- People's physical presence.
- Their emotional and intellectual attention.

In other words, to paraphrase Hallowell, "Turn off your I-Pod, close your laptop, end your daydream, and pay full attention to the other person…and do it in-person!"

The Ability to Respond Appropriately to Emotions

Once you're able to recognize and identify emotions in others, you're ready to work on responding appropriately to those emotions.

As an IT support professional, what is the primary objective of each interaction with your user? The obvious answer is that our objective is to help the user by solving the problem and leaving them with a good feeling about us and our department. Really, nothing else matters.

Interactive Exercise, Part 1

Think about how you have responded *ineffectively* in the past to these emotions in others. Pick two items from the following list and write a brief (one or two sentences) description of how you responded to them.

- Anger

- Hostility

- Sadness

- Jealousy

- Excitement

- Pride

- Nervousness

- Skepticism

Interactive Exercise, Part 2

Now, thinking about the same incidents as in part one of the exercise, think about whether your past responses were the best way to deal with those emotions in others. Write one or two sentences to describe a better way to deal with people who are showing the emotions you selected above.

- Anger

- Hostility

- Sadness

- Jealousy

- Excitement

- Pride

- Nervousness

- Skepticism

The Ability to Control Your Own Emotions

The term "emotional labor" was first defined by the sociologist Arlie Hochschild as the "management of feeling to create a publicly observable facial and bodily display". A good example of emotional labor occurs when a server in a restaurant smiles and expresses positive emotion toward diners. As an IT support professional, you engage in emotional labor when you are pleasant and upbeat with your users.

Figure 4 Emotional labor means putting on your "game" face

Pleasant and Positive

It's easy to be pleasant and positive when you're already in a good mood or when you're dealing with a user who is also pleasant and upbeat. Your challenge comes, however, in being pleasant and positive when you don't feel well, when you're stressed because of personal or work issues, when you're hung-over, or when your user is stressed, argumentative, or generally unpleasant. As an IT support professional, you must put on your "game face" even when you may feel really bad. You can do that by controlling your own emotions.

Successful Servers "Get-It"

Think about restaurant servers. Their income is dependent upon satisfied customers. They understand that their tips are often based on how they make the customer feel. If they complain about things in their life or in the restaurant, it casts a negative aura over the customer's experience and the tipping rate will likely go down. On the other hand, if they create a positive, uplifting experience for the customer, the tipping rate will most likely go up.

> **Always keep things positive and up-beat. Your users will appreciate it and your evaluations will reflect it!**

The Ability to Influence a Desired Emotional Response in Others

Research has discovered what is now being called a "social brain". This social brain actually connects to other social brains. Without going into deep scientific detail, think about the times you've been around other people whose mere presence affected you in one way or another. Some people, when they enter a room, brighten it up. Others cast a cloak of dread. Have you ever been part of a group decision-making process when you felt you knew the outcome of the process just before it was announced? Your

Figure 5 The stoplight metaphor

brain (your social brain) is actually picking up subtle clues from others in the group which tell it how they're thinking and feeling.

In the same way that we can detect the moods of others, we can also influence the moods of others. When we're in a calm state of mind, we can influence others to be in a calm state of mind. Conversely, when we're agitated, we can influence others to become agitated as well.

How to Control Your Own Emotions

Although there are many techniques that can be used to control your emotions and your responses to others' emotions, Goleman suggests one short term and one long term solution. First, the short term solution: Perhaps as a child you were taught, when angry, to count to 10 before doing or saying anything. Good advice. Today, in dealing with kids, there are programs called social/emotional learning. One of the programs uses a stop light metaphor. The kids are told, when they're upset, to remember the stoplight:

- Red: Stop, Calm Down, Think Before You Act
- Yellow: Think of a Range of Things you Can Do
- Green: Choose the Best One

So, the short term solution is to pause and calm yourself before you react, then consider the range of possible responses, and choose the best one.

The long term solution is meditation. Studies have shown that, after as little as eight weeks of meditation, physical changes take place within the brain that help you respond more calmly and appropriately to stressful situations. Meditation doesn't require that you isolate yourself on a mountain top in the Himalayas. There are many forms of meditation including one where you sit quietly with your eyes closed and focus on your breathing for eight minutes a day[2]. Search the web for more information on the myriad forms of meditation. The point is to find ways to generally calm yourself.

---

[2] 8 Minute Meditation: Quiet Your Mind. Change Your Life. by Victor N. Davich, Perigee Trade, 2004

Emotional Intelligence Exercise

Below are the behavioral habits of emotional intelligence. As you read these, rate yourself on each behavioral habit.

Always=5	Usually=4	Sometimes=3	Seldom=2	Almost Never=1
Behavioral Habit				*Score*
1. In all circumstances I respect other people and their feelings.				
2. I can easily identify my feelings.				
3. I take responsibility for my own emotions.				
4. I can maintain control of my emotions.				
5. I find it easy to validate others' feelings and values.				
6. I am non-judgmental of other people and situations.				
7. I don't apply labels to other people.				
8. I do not try to manipulate, criticize, blame, or overpower others.				
9. I constantly challenge my habitual responses, and I am willing to try considered alternatives.				
10. I live in the present, learn from experiences, and do not carry negative feelings forward.				

"Don't believe everything you think."

--Thomas E. Kida

Scoring:

- 44+ = High level of emotional maturity, awareness and control. You have a positive and inspiring impact on others.
- 38-43 = Higher than average level of emotional intelligence. Concentrate on self-awareness and control, and developing increased empathy for others.
- 32-37 = You have a base line awareness of what emotional intelligence is. Be alert for opportunities to increase levels of self-awareness and empathy toward others, and to refine responses.
- 31 or lower = Now that you're of aware of emotional intelligence, monitor your emotions and their impact on you and others. Notice how your behavior affects others. Get feedback on how to modify behaviors with negative effects.

Building Leadership Skills: Leading Teams Winter 2006-2007 - This exercise is based on material created by Andrew Sanderbeck for the Infopeople Project [infopeople.org], supported by the U.S. Institute of Museum and Library Services under the provisions of the Library Services and Technology Act, administered in California by the State Librarian. Any use of this material should credit the author and funding source.

Bonus video: Watch our video on emotional intelligence at www.doncrawley.com/videos

Online EI Resources

Daniel Goleman's website: www.danielgoleman.info

Free emotional intelligence test: www.queendom.com

8 Minute Meditation website: www.8minutes.org

Chapter Four:
What to do When the User Isn't Right

> "Clever men are impressed in their differences from their fellows. Wise men are conscious of their resemblance to them."
>
> –R.H. Tawney

We've all heard the saying, "The customer is always right." The problem is that they're not always right and sometimes they're just downright rude or even abusive. Oddly, when they're so upset that they're rude, we have a chance to turn the situation around. The real problem occurs when they're silently upset and say nothing to us. In retail businesses, only four percent of dissatisfied customers ever say anything. Most of the rest simply quit doing business with the store. A related statistic is that "68 percent of customers quit doing business with a company because of an attitude of *indifference* toward the customer by the owner, manager, or some employee." If we work at an internal help desk we may not be concerned with losing "customers" since our end-users are to some degree a captive audience. In reality they are our customers and when we lose the confidence of those end-users, we may not hear about it, but others in our organization will! They will talk about us behind our back around the water cooler, at the coffee machine, to co-workers and their bosses, and anyone who will listen. What's the risk in that? If we lose their confidence and people start speaking poorly of us behind our backs, we run the risk of losing our jobs to other individuals or through out-sourcing.

Are You Creating Advocates or Detractors?

We can create advocates among our users by delivering outstanding customer service. Advocates speak well of us when we're not around to speak up for ourselves. The opposite occurs when we create detractors by not providing outstanding customer service to our end-users. It's our choice. The actions we choose define our choice.

Warm-up Exercise

Our focus is on working with users to create the best outcome possible for them and for you. To be a savvy IT support person, you need to combine your solid technical expertise with communication skills and other techniques to create a win-win solution for your users and yourself. You will learn how to handle frustrated or angry users, how to project a caring attitude, how to use effective tone-of-voice and body language, how to handle the stress of your job, and how to say no without alienating the end user.

Think back to the Hero/Villain exercise at the beginning of this book. Take a minute to list characteristics of the good support call. Ask yourself these questions:

- What was happening?

- What was the support rep saying? Doing?

- How were you feeling?

- What were you saying, doing?

If you're working with a group, share your observations with the rest of the group members.

Next, think about the bad support situation. Ask yourself the same questions as above:

- What was happening?

- What was the support rep saying? Doing?

- How were you feeling?

- What were you saying, doing?

What makes the difference between a successful support call and an unsuccessful one?

Again, if you're working on this in a group, share your observations with the group.

Who Are Your Users?

One of the biggest challenges you face as an IT support person is dealing with users who become angry and want to take their frustrations out on you. On top of a busy schedule, hard-to-solve technical problems, and pressure, you are sometimes faced with an unreasonable person, who despite your best efforts, ends up being angry not only at the situation but also at you.

Users are your customers. Their happiness is your concern because you are paid to help them solve their problems. In order to keep your job and enjoy what you are doing, you need to earn the respect of your users. When they respect you, they pay attention to your advice. When they don't respect you, they will ignore you, or complain that you are not helpful.

Even if users are wrong or demanding, you must learn how to treat them with respect, courtesy, and professionalism. You might think that it sounds unfair that you have to work extra hard to appease the user when the user is wrong or out of control. But until users know you care about them and their situation, they will not be able to appreciate your knowledge and problem-solving skills. If you want to be treated well, you need to seek to understand your users, uncover their motivations, and connect with their desired outcome.

"…people don't care how much you know until they know how much you care."

–Dr. Martin Luther King, Jr.

What is Your User Angry About?

It is sometimes said that anger is the only emotion that does not stand alone. What do you think this means?" Anger usually results from or masks another emotion.

What are some other emotions that might result in an angry user?

The real issue(s) are often below
the surface and not obvious

Figure 6 The iceberg of anger

A user can become upset or seem angry for a number of reasons. You have no way of knowing what happened to the user immediately before you encountered him or her. For example, she may have just received bad news about a close family member, he may have just received divorce papers, she may have just received a bad diagnosis from a doctor, or any of myriad other things that could affect his or her emotions and behavior. Sometimes, even though the anger seems directed at you, it may, in fact, have nothing (or little) to do with you.

To be able to identify underlying emotions is to understand the user better. This is a good skill to acquire and will improve your ability to diffuse the user's anger and move on to resolve his or her technical issue. Not only will the ability to understand users improve your IT support work, this sensitivity will also be useful in all aspects of your life.

First Steps

It is often necessary to appease the user before you fix the technical problem. This may take several tools that you need to arm yourself with: listening with empathy, apologizing when necessary, and headlining to create a satisfied user. Sensitivity to the user is important because it helps us deliver bad news in an acceptable way. It all goes back to empathy – walking a mile in our user's shoes. Often, a successful support session involves negotiating an acceptable outcome. Negotiating with a user is most successful when you use a win-win approach.

Your skill in handling their problem and the words you choose are the keys to keeping good relations with your users and being able to work with them to their satisfaction. Angry users present an opportunity to create loyal and supportive users if you don't let them ruin your day. It starts with identifying what users want from their IT staff, and then making sure that you are delivering what they want using your best skills.

What Users Want

Take a minute to make a list of what you are looking for when you call for help or support on a product or service. What is important to you? Users care about the same things you do when they contact you for assistance. They want:

Dependable and reliable service

This means providing reliable and accurate service - consistently accurate answers and follow-through on your promises. Users should get the same courteous, pleasant and knowledgeable service every time they contact the IT staff.

To accomplish this, consider adopting the tactic of under-promising so you can over-deliver. In other words, set expectations with your user at a reasonable level, but one at which you can consistently exceed their expectations. That means giving yourself and your co-workers a cushion when making promises to users. For example, if you need to research a problem for a user, and you think you can call them back in two hours, discipline yourself to tell the user that you will get back to them in, for example, four hours. This helps account for unexpected emergencies that might come up, yet still permits you meet your user's expectations. Using this technique, your users will be wowed, and you will reduce your personal stress.

Responsiveness

Responsiveness is the willingness to respond to user needs by answering their phone or email requests quickly, and being willing to do what it takes to respond effectively to a service request.

Responsiveness is adopting a can-do attitude, and a willingness to go the extra mile for the user. Recent industry trends indicate that soft skills (such as listening, empathy, courtesy and creating rapport) are as or more important than technical skills in the career advancement of any employee. This is especially true in the support industry, where most managers have realized that they must hire people who have a good attitude or approach to serving customers (users) plus an aptitude for technical knowledge, and that the rest can be taught.

A positive attitude is the first step in building good soft skills. You have control over your attitude. Just like you can choose what clothes to wear in the morning, you can also choose what attitude to assume every day. Although it has become a cliché, it is true that you can choose to see the glass as half-full, or half-empty. Your approach, or attitude, toward life is a self-fulfilling prophecy. If your attitude is "Each day is a journey filled with interesting activities and challenges!", then you will interpret everything that happens to you in a positive light. On the other hand, if you approach your job and your life in a less than positive way, every bump in the road will seem like a huge obstacle.

Take a few minutes to ask yourself the following questions.

1. Do I put myself in my user's shoes?

2. Do I take ownership of a problem and see it through to completion?

3. Am I willing to help both users and co-workers?

4. Do I consciously assume a positive outlook with users and co-workers?

5. Am I respectful and courteous to the user?

6. Do I treat everyone with respect and courtesy?

7. Do I speak and conduct myself confidently with users?

If you answered yes to at least five, you are on the right track to creating a positive position from which to serve your users for the best results. If you answered yes to fewer than five, your attitude might be keeping you from doing your best to create the proper environment for success in your job. Frankly, your attitude may be keeping you from achieving career success.

Competence

Competence means providing correct, knowledgeable service, performed with accuracy and confidence. Here are a couple of good techniques to use to demonstrate your competence.

Tell your user what you are going to do before you do it. This technique is called headlining, in the sense that a newspaper article's headline tells you what you are going to read before you read it. As a user, it is very frustrating to be dealing with a service provider who does not tell you what he or she is doing. When there is silence on the phone, the user may be confused or concerned that he has been disconnected, and this does not assure the user of your competence. You know you have not done a good job of headlining if, after a period of silence, your user says, "Are you still there?" The user does not feel cared for if she has to guess if you are still on the line.

Headlining is the mark of a professional IT support provider. It is easy and quick to do, and creates a high degree of user satisfaction. Use headlining when you need to take a moment to look up some information in the database. You can say, "It will take me just a minute to look that up in the database." This gives the user the assurance that you are working on her/him behalf.

If the problem is going to require more than just a few minutes, give your user the option of getting a call back from you instead of being on hold or listening to you work for an extended period of time. (Make sure to call him/her back when you say you will!)

Another way of providing assurance to users is to build their confidence in your ability to help them. This can be done with a solution statement delivered once you understand and have confirmed the user's problem. A solution statement simply tells the user that you can help them solve the problem. You can say, "From what you have told me, I know how to solve the problem."

Examples of Competence Statements

- "This is going to take me a moment. I'm not ignoring you." About every 20 to 30 seconds, say something like "I'm still working on it." or "I'm still here. I haven't forgotten you."
- "I dealt with something similar recently. I can take care of that for you."

Empathy

Empathy means providing caring and personal service. Support personnel convey empathy when they listen for the hidden meaning in what a user is saying, acknowledge the emotion, and offer caring assistance.

Empathy is especially important when dealing with a user who is irritated, angry or emotional. When we are emotional, it is difficult for us to act rationally. This is because of the way our brains are structured. Our emotional brain, which is a relatively primitive part of the human brain, in essence "hijacks" the rest of our more rational, analytical brain and takes control.

To get someone out of the grip of the emotional brain and pass the power over to the analytical brain takes one of three things:

1. Intervention of a skilled listener or support professional

2. Concerted effort on the part of the emotional person

3. Passing of time

It is important to understand this as we deal with emotional, upset or angry users. Empathy is a remedy for calming an emotional person by simply acknowledging the emotion that the user feels. Empathy is very powerful because it diffuses emotion. If you want to be able to deal rationally with an emotional user, or if you simply want to ensure that an interaction does not escalate into an emotional one, remember to use empathy. If sincerely applied, it works like a charm in most situations.

Examples of Empathy Statements

- "I can hear how frustrated you are."

- "I can see how that would annoy you."

- "That's terrible!"

- "I understand how time-critical this is."

- "I would be unhappy if that happened to me, too."

Professionalism

Professionalism means that how you speak and act and the emails or other materials you send reflect a high level of training and expertise. This becomes the professional image that you project to your users.

Here are some ways you can project a professional image to users on the phone:

Smile

A smile on your face affects how your voice sounds on the phone. Smiling creates more pleasant resonance in a phone voice and is the first step in conveying a professional image. Maybe you've heard the phrase, "Smile and dial!" Some professionals who use the phone place mirrors at their desks so they can check their smile before talking on the phone.

Approach each interaction with a positive attitude

We know how a positive attitude is self-fulfilling. Your users deserve a cheerful approach on every interaction. IT support personnel must perform extreme self-care in order to approach each phone call positively. If you feel you cannot be positive on the next phone call, ask your manager for a few minutes to take a walk or get a bite to eat. Your users will be grateful that you took a break so you can return with a fresh attitude.

Speak clearly

Mumbling conveys a lack of confidence. Enunciating and speaking in a clear, moderate tone of voice conveys confidence and professionalism. Listen carefully to yourself speak and you will be amazed how much better your annunciation becomes. You will also pay more attention to the words you use.

Develop rapport

Being "in rapport" means being in sync with your user's communication style. Have you ever instantly liked someone you were talking to over the phone, even though you had not met them and do not know them personally? Chances are that you were in rapport with them. They may have been using some techniques that are very effective to make you feel at home with them.

Mirroring is a subtle way to conform your behavior to match the behavior of your user. It is the genuine search for areas of similarity between you and your communication partner, and its purpose is to make people feel comfortable with you. There are several auditory ways to create rapport through mirroring on the phone:

Never refer to your user with overly familiar or condescending nicknames such as:

- Dude
- Bud
- Honey
- Sweetie
- Buddy
- Pal
- Son
- Young man
- Young lady
- Old man
- Old lady

- Matching your rate of speech and the tone of your voice to that of the user

- Using the same verbal expressions and repeating or paraphrasing what the user has said

If the user is speaking slowly and you normally speak very quickly, moderate your normal rate of speech. If your user is using a loud voice, speak up just a bit. Remember, you do not want to mirror the aggressive behavior or anger of a user. If the user uses an incorrect technical term, use the same language at first and then gently educate the user by saying "We also call that the file extension."

Repeating or paraphrasing is an excellent way to mirror the user's communication style. It is also a powerful listening technique. A good time to use paraphrasing is when you are asking a series of questions while troubleshooting. You can repeat or paraphrase a few key words of the user's answer to confirm your understanding.

Avoid slang, colloquialisms, profanity and terms of endearment

People from other parts of the country or the world may not understand some of the terms you may use when speaking casually to your friends. IT support personnel should always use professional language in speaking to users. Professional language does not include profanity, terms of endearment, or slang nicknames such as dude, bud, honey, sweetie, buddy, or pal, or other forms of slang. An exception to this rule is when speaking with a user with whom you have a personal relationship, but a wise IT support person will still exercise caution when communicating with any user.

Flow for Handling User Calls

Here is a flow to a support interaction that you can use to make sure your calls and written communications go the way you want them to. Following these steps will ensure that you give the best customer service as you resolve user issues. It will also help you to diffuse users who are angry or upset.

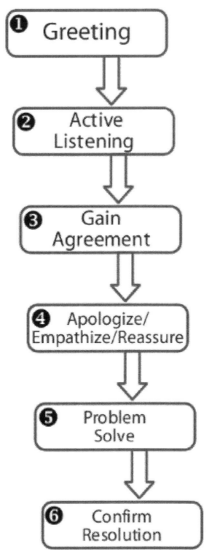

Figure 7 Flow for handling user calls and visits

1: Greeting

Start off your phone call or site visit with a greeting that is sincere yet inviting. Your greeting, the first time your caller hears your voice, sets the tone for the rest of the conversation. The first impression is the one that lasts. You want to be inviting and sound interested in what the caller has to say. If you approach each call with a genuine desire to help, your sincerity will come through in the tone and quality of your voice and your words will be heard and appreciated. You will be setting the stage for a good outcome.

Be careful about using a lengthy, canned greeting such as, "Gigantacorp Computer Services Help Desk, where we always strive for top-rated service. This is Tom Helpful, MCDST, CCNA. How may I provide you with excellent service this fine morning?" Something more appropriate is, "Computer Services Help Desk. This is Tom. May I help you?"

Just in Case You Get Disconnected

Shortly after your initial greeting, be sure to get a call-back number for your user in case the call gets disconnected.

2: Active listening

When you actively listen you are demonstrating to your user that you hear what they are saying and you are taking in the important information they are providing you about their issue. Use verbal cues, such as "all right,", "okay," "I see," and "I understand." You will also need to deliver them with empathy and understanding in your voice. You would not want to respond to a user with a dry, uncaring tone of voice. This would most likely cause frustration for the user.

3: Gain agreement

Gaining agreement with the user on why they are contacting you is an important part of the overall user support process. Gaining agreement is paraphrasing or reflecting back what you believe to be the user's problem. Taking time to gain agreement gives you an opportunity to check your understanding of the situation so that you address the correct issue to your user's satisfaction.

Examples of Gaining Agreement with the User

"So you are trying to create a PDF and the graphics don't look right. Is this the main issue you are calling about today?"

"So what we need to focus on today is finding out why your new laptop battery charge is so weak. Is that correct?"

Sometimes, it might be necessary to say things like, "I'd like to just quickly go through a check list to make sure I completely understand the issue. Some of the things may seem obvious, but I want to make sure I don't overlook anything. Is it okay to go through the checklist with you?"

Once you have gained agreement, your user may still be a little frustrated, but feeling more comfortable because of the professionalism and empathy you have displayed so far.

4: Apologize/Empathize/Reassure

After you gain agreement, it is important to let the user know that the frustration or disappointment they are experiencing is justified and understandable. For example, "I think anyone in your situation would be frustrated or "I can understand why you are disappointed at this time." Acknowledging feelings helps the user know that they are justified in their frustration.

Reassurance fosters confidence and trust by assuring the user that you will do whatever you can to help! Reassure the user that you will do your best to resolve their issue as quickly as possible.

An Example of How to Show Empathy and Reassure

"Okay, so I understand the situation to be that you finally convinced your boss to get you a new laptop because you needed a more reliable machine for all the travel you have been doing lately. You got the new laptop, and now the battery won't hold a charge. I think anyone in your situation would be very dissatisfied at this point. Let me assure you, you have reached the right place! Let me see what I can do to help."

In the preceding example, the exact words are probably different from the words that you would choose. The point is not the verbiage, but the underlying message which includes agreement on the problem, empathy, and reassurance.

At this point, your user will likely be much more flexible and willing to seek resolution through troubleshooting than they were when they first contacted you. By this time, the user is probably going to thank you. They realize at this moment that they are with a competent, caring, intelligent technical support person who is actually going to help them resolve the situation. The next step would be to consider whether an apology is in order.

Apologize, if necessary. Your user would like an apology for the less than satisfactory situation they are in, regardless of who is at fault. It's human nature. You should apologize when:

- You have made a mistake.
- Someone else has made a mistake.
- The failure of a product or service frustrates the user.

An example of an appropriate apology is: "I am sorry that your laptop battery is defective."

Of course, a sincere expression of sympathy for another person's difficult situation is always appropriate.

5: Problem Solve

Remember how, when you call for help with an order or support with a product, you want to talk to someone who takes a genuine interest in you and your situation. You want results. When you take on the user's problem or situation and work it as if it were your own, you will be providing outstanding customer service. Everything about your interaction with the caller will be genuine and positive. You will be creative when needed, taking into account exactly what the user has told you and trying your best to work toward a solution. Being a problem solver means that you treat someone the way you like to be treated, using all of your knowledge and skills to improve the caller's situation or dilemma. You go the extra step to research and implement the best solution. No matter what you are able to do for them, your users will feel that they have been treated well, and will trust you and pay attention to the advice you give them. When you approach each interaction by giving it your full attention, you will receive positive feedback and be appreciated for your work – even when you can't do exactly what the user asks you to do.

Order Matters!

Isn't it interesting how the problem-solving process is the next to the last step? The steps leading up to problem-solving ensure that you understand what the problem is and that the user is confident of your ability to solve his or her problem.

6: Confirm Resolution
The last phase is confirmation that the problem is indeed resolved. That's where you ask if the problem is resolved to the user's satisfaction. Do not close the ticket until the user confirms that the issue is resolved to her or his satisfaction. If there's time and the user doesn't seem to be in a rush, you can ask the other two questions that

go at the end of a support session, which are, "Are you satisfied with the way I handled your problem?" and "Is there anything I could have done better?" If the user seems to be in a hurry, don't ask the last two questions, but you must always, always, always ask the first question to get confirmation of resolution before hanging up and closing the ticket.

What about in-person support calls instead of on the telephone? Well, the same six steps still apply. You still have to offer a friendly, professional greeting. You must still do active listening and gain agreement to ensure you correctly understand the issue. You'll still apologize/empathize/reassure. You've still got to problem solve and you certainly don't want to leave without confirming that the problem is resolved.

Whether it's on the phone, in person, in a chat session, or even in email, following these six steps will ensure you manage the support ticket or situation in a professional manner that will reflect well on you and your department.

Bonus Video: Watch the video about the Six Steps in a Successful Support Call at www.doncrawley.com/videos

Interactive Exercise: Role Play with an Upset User

Work with a partner on this exercise. Each of you should think of a real-life customer service problem you can role-play. Take turns being the end user and the IT support person.

Sample Scenarios

- "My taskbar keeps disappearing."
- "Why is my computer so slow?"
- "I was working on a large report for my boss. I'm sure I saved the file, but I can't find it anywhere."

You should come up with enough detail to talk for about three minutes. You may want to jot down notes or create a practice script.

Begin the first role-play. When five minutes are up, have the person who was playing the role of the user give feedback to the person who was the support person. Repeat the process, switching roles.

Take turns calling with your problem. IT support person – use your best communication skills to diffuse the situation, keep the call on track, and resolve the issue for user satisfaction.

When you are finished, users should give the IT support person feedback on how she or he did using the techniques we just learned, including the flow for handling user calls. Use the questions on the following page.

Evaluate the Role Play

1. Did your user feel good about what you said and how you reacted to their problem? Get their feedback on how you came across.

2. How did you demonstrate that you were listening?

3. Did your tone of voice reflect sincere empathy? How do you know? Did you use mirroring?

4. Did you acknowledge your user's feelings? What was their response or reaction?

5. How were you reassuring?

6. What did you learn from this experience?

Chapter Five:
The Art of Listening Well

"The body says what words cannot."
--Martha Graham
US choreographer and dancer

The Five Levels of Listening

Communications experts say that we listen at five different and distinct levels. How you listen to your users will have a significant impact on your success, and that of the overall IT support team.

Ignoring

The lowest level of listening is called ignoring – not listening at all. If you are distracted by anything while talking to a user, they can get the impression that you are ignoring them. For example, while the user is speaking, you start a conversation or interject a comment with another IT support tech. You are ignoring your user.

Pretend Listening

Pretend listening is most easily explained in the face-to-face conversation. You're talking to the other person and they have that "backpacking in Brazil" look in their eyes. On the phone it happens when you say things like "I see" and "OK," etc. while working on an unrelated email or playing a computer game. People can tell you're distracted.

Selective Listening

During selective listening we pay attention to the speaker as long as they are talking about things we like or agree with. If they move on to other things we slip down to pretend listening or ignore them altogether.

Attentive Listening

Attentive listening occurs when we carefully listen to the other person, but while they are speaking we are deciding whether we agree or disagree, determining whether they are right or wrong.

At all four of these levels it should be evident that we are listening to our own perspective, and in most cases with the intent to respond from our experience.

Empathic Listening

To be successful in providing IT support to end users, you must teach yourself to treat every call as though this is the first time you've ever heard this problem, even though you may have heard it many times before. Discipline yourself to see it through the eyes of the user. This is called empathic listening. Empathic listening is the highest level of listening, and the hardest to accomplish.

Where is your focus?

As you think about the five levels of listening, think about the fact that the first four levels are self-focused, while the fifth level (empathic listening) is focused on the user. When your focus is completely on the user and not on yourself, your level of service will be much higher.

Bonus Video: Watch the video about the Five Levels of Listening at www.doncrawley.com/videos

How to Achieve Empathic Listening

What's Your Hurry? Be Patient.

Users who are rushed will be annoyed, not satisfied. They will feel that they did not get top notch service. Slow down. Assess your user's urgency. What is your user's availability? What is your user's timeframe? What is your user's mood?

A user may not be able to fully articulate the problem, and may stumble over an explanation, or take a long-winded approach to explaining what is wrong. Allow the caller to have time to finish the explanation. An issue that the user mentions casually may be important. The caller will appreciate that you took the extra time to listen and get involved, going the extra step to be helpful.

It's easy to place blame on the technology, the tools, other departments, a service provider, the management, the company or the organization, or the user. Be a problem solver, not a blamer.

Talk Less and Listen More

> "Courage is what it takes to stand up and speak; courage is also what it takes to sit down and listen."
>
> --Winston Churchill

Users are very important people. They are the reason you have a job. They deserve your undivided attention and your most gracious approach to problem-solving. You may know more than they do on the reason for their call, but you will only win when your user is satisfied.

Listen to everything your user says, as if there is going to be a test at the end of the conversation. Empathize with her problems and issues. Jot down notes and ideas to respond to, without losing your attention. Make comments to acknowledge his problem and position. Repeat the points your user made in your own words (paraphrase) to make sure you understand and to let her know she has been heard.

Be careful not to use technical jargon and acronyms your user doesn't understand. You could confuse, intimidate, or anger him. By empathically listening to your user you will be able to detect her level of expertise. You can also politely ask her how technical she would like you to be. In the same way that a less technically-oriented user could get intimidated or angry by overly technical explanations, a more technically-oriented user could get frustrated or angry by overly simple explanations (or a condescending attitude on your part). Be sensitive to whom you're speaking with. Regardless of her level of technical competence, make sure you have given her permission to interrupt you and ask for an explanation or clarification if she is confused by your explanation.

At the end of the call, do a short recap of what you have discussed, what approach you are suggesting, and any follow up on your part or the user's part that is needed. Be specific about how you will follow up, what you will do, and what the he can expect and when it will happen.

Ten Keys to Being a Good Listener

1. Stop talking.
2. Lose distractions including internal distractions from your mental clutter of things like to-do lists and plans for the weekend and external distractions such as cell phones, computers, and open books.
3. Focus on what the other person is saying as though there will be a test at the end of the conversation.
4. Keep your mind open to the possibility of new information. Try not to let your personal beliefs close your mind to new ideas.
5. Use physical and verbal responses, appropriate timed, to show you're listening such as nodding your head, raising your eyebrows, saying "uh-huh", and "oh".
6. Let the other person finish what he or she is saying. Resist the temptation to jump in with your response.
7. Ask questions for clarification as needed, but only after letting the other person finish.

> ### Create a Human Moment
>
> Remember Hallowell's "Human Moment" from earlier in the book?
>
> Put down the iPad and cell phone, turn off the computer, close the book, abandon the daydream, and focus on the other person!

8. Repeat back what the other person said. You can say things like, "I want to be sure I understand you, so please let me repeat back what you just said." Then repeat back what you think was said and say, "Is that correct? Is that the message you wanted to convey?"
9. Silence or a pause in the conversation does not necessarily mean you have to jump in and speak right away. Sometimes, you're better off allowing silence while you process what you've just heard.
10. Be sensitive to the non-verbal cues.

Chapter Six:
Making Sure They Know You Care

> "Positive thoughts yield positive language yield positive results."
>
> –Paul R. Senness

Making Sure They Know You Care

Remember the previously quoted study that 68% of customers are lost due to perceived indifference? In a busy IT department, we sometimes forget that providing excellent service involves more than just fixing the problem. Outstanding service includes making users feel good about their interaction with you by quickly creating a human bond.

The Three Components of Communication

- Words

- Tone of voice

- Non-verbal cues

When you can hear and see the person you are talking to your message is composed of words, tone of voice, and non-verbal cues (or body-language). An often quoted research study by Albert Mehrabian (currently Professor Emeritus of Psychology, UCLA) suggests, when conveying feelings or attitudes, that words carry 7% of the message impact and tone of voice carries 38%. That means the body language conveys 55% of the message impact. (The study has come to be known as the 7%-38%-55% rule.) Although the study dealt with communicating emotions and attitudes, the fundamental concept of body language as an important element of communication can also be applied to other forms of communication. The point is that body language plays a large role in how messages are communicated. Another point of the study is that your non-verbals need to be consistent with your verbal communication in order for you to have credibility with your listener. Imagine the confusion that might exist if you say to someone, "I'm really interested in hearing what you have to say." while you're typing text messages on your phone. There's a huge disconnect between the message communicated by the words coming out of your mouth and the message communicated by your actions.

> What you do speaks so loudly that I cannot hear what you say.
> --Ralph Waldo Emerson

It would be inaccurate to say that when you are on the phone most of the message impact is missing because we all imagine what the other person is doing and looks like – and the professionalism (or lack of it) can heavily influence that perception. It is incumbent upon the IT support professional to create an atmosphere that convinces the user that you are sitting beside them as a teammate. Here are some golden rules to follow to create a satisfying experience for yourself and the user.

Use Gentle Humor

Caution: Humor can offend when you don't expect it. Avoid topics like sex, race, religion, politics, or anything in poor taste. Remember, your job is the provide IT support, not to be a comedian.

Most people prefer dealing with people who enjoy themselves. Display a cheerful sense of humor coupled with good judgment and common sense. Laughing at yourself is usually safe, but unless you know the individual with whom you are working, tread lightly on other forms of humor.

A few users will want to just take care of business. For them user service is quick, efficient, get down to business, with a good attitude. Always respect your user's time; when they're in a hurry, just deliver the service with pleasant professionalism!

Of course, we're human and it's difficult to avoid using your own help desk humor with your co-workers and friends. Some of your work stories are guaranteed to entertain when used in the right circumstances. IT support desk humor is born from the tension between knowledgeable "power users" like yourselves, who staff IT support desks, and the users who call in. Avoid, however, sharing such humor with end users. Something you consider funny might have actually happened to the person who calls in and she/he might have found it embarrassing. If you bring it up in an attempt to be funny, you could cause that person to relive an embarrassing moment.

What is Funny to Some May Be Painful to Another

I don't normally teach end-user classes, but a client had an emergency situation and needed someone to teach a basic Excel class. They asked me to do it and, since they were an excellent client, I agreed. During the class, I made a joke about someone being confused by asterisks being displayed in a password field instead of the actual password. Most of the people laughed, but at the break one individual came up to me nearly in tears. She explained that she had been confused by the asterisks and felt that everyone was laughing at her. You might think she was overreacting, but it doesn't really matter whether she was or wasn't. What matters is that my actions unintentionally (and unnecessarily) caused another human being pain. Since that time, I've tried to be more sensitive to how my choice of words and humor might affect another person. If I were a comedian whose job is to make people laugh, I might feel differently, but I'm a teacher and my job is to educate. I need to be very careful of anything that gets in the way of doing my job. Similarly, our jobs as IT support staff are to support end-users and help them work more effectively, creatively, and productively. We also need to be very careful of anything that gets in the way of doing our jobs.

Always be respectful of your users, even when you don't think they can hear what you say. Things said about someone have a way of getting back to that individual.

Never Pretend You Know What You Are Doing

Users call in assuming you will instantly have the right answer. Recognize that no one is a fully qualified expert and that you too have a lot to learn. Know your limits. You may not have all the answers, but you do have a set of customer service tools. Using all of the support tools will make you look competent and confident.

Dr. Stephen R. Covey, author of The 7 Habits of Highly Effective People, says that we all have a personality ethic and a character ethic. The personality ethic is what people see on the surface, much like what's above the water line of an iceberg. The character ethic lies deep beneath. If your personality is not buoyed up by strong character you can come off as a phony. Perhaps not at first, but eventually the user will perceive the truth. The success and reputation of the IT department rests on the user's experience. If this trust gets broken through a "know it all" attitude it will be a long road back to credibility. It is one thing to speak with a tone of authority and confidence, but something entirely different to come off as a "know-it-all". Remember, you will gain far more respect from your users with a "Let me research that and get back to you" correct answer than with an expedient incorrect answer that may cause damage to the user's work, and will damage the IT support center's reputation.

Sometimes you can't fulfill what the user is asking for. Instead of saying no, focus on what you can do. Use "I can, will, do, yes, you bet, absolutely." There are a couple of ways we can do this. Users don't expect you to be perfect. They do expect you to be honest. If you make a mistake, acknowledge it, apologize for it, fix it and move on.

The Power of Positive

There are two self-fulfilling prophecies. One is "positive thoughts yield positive language yield positive results." It means that when we think about things (our job, our abilities, our users, and other aspects of our life) in a positive way, we tend to talk about those things in positive manner. A result of this is that we attract more positive results. The opposite end of the spectrum is also true – "negative thoughts yield negative language yield negative results." Think about these two approaches to life and the impact they have had on your experiences. Which approach puts you at ease and which puts you on edge? Which approach left you satisfied and which led to unhappiness? We are in control of and can choose our attitude. That choice significantly impacts not only our mood and outlook, but also that of everyone around us and those with whom we come in contact.

Of course, this doesn't mean every day will be nothing but fun. There will be hard and frustrating days and events. The decisions you make in how to approach such challenges will determine the outcome and future for both you and your user.

Here are some tips to create the positive climate we all like to respond to:

Help the User Find a Workaround

Sometimes you have to be a creative solution provider.

- No email? Try a co-worker's computer, use web mail, a personal account as a temporary solution while we fix your office email account.
- Can't print? Ask a co-worker?
- No shared access to something? Can you get in and email it to them?
- Is a failed router or firewall preventing Internet access? Is there a coffee shop nearby? What about an Internet-enabled phone?

Working with Workarounds

How have you used your creativity in finding workarounds? If you're working in a group, share what you have done on the job to help users when regular solutions failed.

How did this make you feel?

How did your user react?

What kinds of workarounds have you found for yourself in the past?

Partner With Your User

Become co-owner of the problem. Use "we" statements instead of "you". Let your user vent when necessary. Even if the user says "don't bother", do it anyway, and follow up with them. They will appreciate it.

Be a Valuable Resource

Instead of being the one who knows all and can fix anything, be the one who will find the best answer, see the problem through to a solution, and focus on what users can do for themselves. Help them to get it done so they will feel good about the interaction. Most of us like to be self-sufficient. Anytime you can teach your users to be self-sufficient, they will increase their skills, cut down on the need to call you again, and feel empowered. By empowering your users, you are creating user satisfaction and a positive outcome.

Teamwork

Share ideas and solutions with your co-workers. You may be able to share knowledge or tidbits with them and they may be able to help you learn something you don't know.

Do One More Thing

Whenever you feel that the user has reached a point where s/he is satisfied, do one more thing. It doesn't have to be anything big. Just a little something extra you can do for them or assistance you can provide makes all the difference.

A "Baker's Dozen" is 13, or one more than a conventional dozen. There are several theories about where the concept originated, but what really matters is the idea of giving your customers (or users) more than they expect.

A Loving Approach to Ceramics

Kristin Love is a successful ceramic artist. She creates her own unique pieces of pottery and sells them through various channels including the Internet (http://www.loveartworks.net). Kristin believes in the "baker's dozen". When you buy an item from her, she always includes a little something extra. The bonus items are not large or expensive, but their perceived value as a token of appreciation is huge. Imagine the customers delight at receiving a special surprise with their order!

How do you provide a "baker's dozen" to your users?

As an IT support staffer, you're not in a position to include an extra item in the shipping box, but you can find ways of providing extra touches for your users. Here are some ideas:

- At the end of a support session, share a new keyboard shortcut you've just discovered
- Send a follow up email a week after a support session asking how things are going
- Based on your knowledge of how a user works, send an email offering a shortcut or tip chosen especially for that user
- Send a handwritten thank you note to a user for using your IT support services. Include your business card in the envelope.

Important note: Always be sensitive to your user's situation. For example, if your user is obviously under a deadline or otherwise in a hurry, just deliver the service, ask if you've solved the problem and if there is anything else the user wants, thank her, and excuse yourself. You can always go back to the user at a more convenient time to deliver the extra bits of service.

Lagniappe (pronounced LAN-yap) is a small gift given to a customer at the time of a purchase. It is a term mainly associated with Louisiana, but it is applicable worldwide. Lagniappe is that little something extra. What are you giving your users (your customers) for lagniappe?

Call Example #1

Read through the transcript of this support call. Analyze the effectiveness of this interaction by answering the questions that follow the transcript. Be prepared to share your insights.

IT Support Staffer: "IT"

User: "Hi, I'm having trouble getting my reports to print out."

IT Support Staffer: "Employee number?"

User: "Sure, it's 123456. I'm wondering - is it me or the computer that is causing the problem?"

IT Support Staffer: {long silence} "What module are you looking at?"

User: "Well, it's the A/R module of the financial package. I'm running the aging report, and I can see it on the screen, but it won't print. I'm really beginning to wonder if my computer is jinxed!"

IT Support Staffer: {long silence} "OK, bud, it's fixed now. Call back if it doesn't work?"

User: "OK, well, I guess that's OK. I'll call back if it isn't working. Bye."

IT Support Staffer: "Later."

Call Example #1 Analysis

Was the problem fixed to the user's satisfaction?

Did the IT support staffer's approach show professionalism?

Did the IT support staffer take advantage of opportunities to connect with the user?

How do you think the IT support staffer's approach came across to the user? What techniques were used?

Did the IT support staffer do the best job possible during this interaction?

If not, what could be done differently?

Call Example #2

Read through the transcript of this new and improved support call. Analyze the effectiveness of this interaction by answering the questions that follow the transcript. Be prepared to share your insights.

IT Support Staffer: "Computer Services. This is Sean How may I help you?"

User: "Hi, I'm having trouble getting my reports to print out."

IT Support Staffer: "That's strange. I'd be glad to help you with that problem, and I need to start with some basics. Can I have your employee number so I can look up your record?"

User: "Sure, it's 123456. I'm wondering - is it me or the computer that is causing the problem?"

IT Support Staffer: (chuckling) "Well, I sometimes wonder that same thing about my car in the morning. Could you tell me what module you are looking at?"

User: "Well, it's the A/R module of the financial package. I'm running the aging report and I can see it on the screen, but it won't print. I'm really beginning to wonder if my computer is jinxed!"

IT Support Staffer: "I doubt that the computer is jinxed, because I can see that the printer queue is stalled and it looks like I can start it from here. Give me just a moment, please. I'm not ignoring you. (Silence for about 20 seconds) OK, it's fixed now. Why don't you try it while I'm on the phone to make sure it's working?"

User: OK, well, here goes. Oh, great – here comes the report! Wow, that's great.

You've been a terrific help. Thanks."

IT Support Staffer: "My pleasure. Is there anything else I can help with today?"

User: "No, I'm all set. And thanks again."

IT Support Staffer: "You're welcome. Call whenever you need us. Goodbye."

Call Example #2 Analysis

Was the problem fixed to the user's satisfaction?

Did the IT support staffer's approach show professionalism?

Did the IT support staffer take advantage of opportunities to connect

with the user? What techniques were used?

How do you think the IT support staffer's approach came across to the

user?

How do you use these techniques in your own IT support work?

Chapter Seven:
Communicating through Email, Texting, and Instant Messaging

"Diamonds are forever. E-mail comes close."

June Kronholz
Wall Street Journal
Education Correspondent

Communicating Through Email

Email is often the most commonly used form of communication for IT support professionals. Email is a one-dimensional form of communication which, although efficient, fails to account for human emotions as a vital component of communication.

In order for your user to know you care, you must follow several important rules when communicating via email.

Here are some rules for using email appropriately to support your users (many of these tips also apply to live chat or texting sessions):

1. Use a descriptive and specific subject line that will help you and the user identify this particular email conversation in the future. Many support ticketing systems automatically add a ticket number. If yours doesn't, consider adding a ticket number manually.
2. Personalize your response by including the user's name.
3. Re-read the sender's original email to ensure that you're answering all of his questions and haven't inadvertently overlooked any of the issues in the email.
4. Never assume that the user has a particular level of knowledge. It is much better to be too thorough than to omit necessary steps because you assume the user already knows something.
5. Anticipate related issues that the user might have and include links to support pages or, if necessary, steps for the user to follow if she encounters any related issues.
6. Bullet-point your response to make it easier to read.
7. If your response includes step-by-step instructions, be sure to number them. If you're creating such instructions from scratch, be sure to test them to ensure you haven't omitted any steps or made false assumptions about how the steps should work.
8. Show professionalism by using proper grammar and avoiding the use of texting shortcuts (they're fine for personal use, but have no place in business)

9. Additionally, show professionalism by proofreading for meaning, spelling, grammar, and mechanical errors such as repeated keystrokes or incorrect spelling corrections (just get in the habit of re-reading every email completely before hitting the send button).

10. Use emoticons to express or to clarify emotions (but be careful about their overuse).

11. Make sure your contact information is included in every email. Automated signature features in most email programs make this very easy. Include your name, phone number, email address, office hours, and appropriate links such as your company or department website, support pages, and any work-related social networking sites such as LinkedIn.

Email Support Examples

Notice in the first screen capture how the support person seems to take a cavalier attitude toward the user and her problem. He displays unprofessionalism by using abbreviations, poor grammar (spelling "your" when he means "you're"), assuming she knows how to make the change to IMAP, and not providing contact information.

Figure 8 A really bad email response to a support ticket

95

In the following examples, the support staffer follows the above rules by:

- providing a descriptive subject line
- calling the user by name
- repeating back his understanding of the problem
- anticipating other problems (such as the program not being installed)
- using headers to segment the problem resolution sections
- numbering the steps
- using an emoticon to relieve any possible anxiety over the word "advanced"
- providing contact information including office hours
- providing a website with additional information.

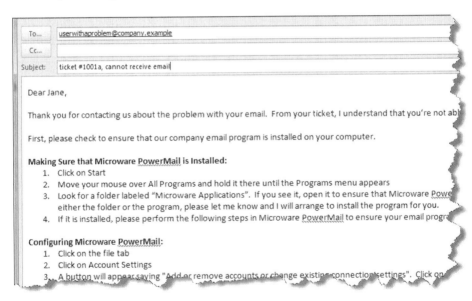

Figure 9 The top half of a good email response

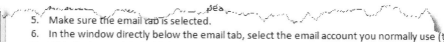

5. Make sure the email tab is selected.
6. In the window directly below the email tab, select the email account you normally use (t
7. Click the button labeled "Change".
8. Click on the button labeled "Advanced" (don't worry, it's not really advanced! ☺)
9. Beside the words "Mail Server Setting" is a pull-down menu including POP3 and IMAP.
10. Choose IMAP and click "Save".
11. Click "Close".
12. Try sending and receiving email.
13. Please let me know if it works or not by replying to this email or calling me at (206) 555-12

I hope this is helpful for you. Anytime you need us, we're here for you.

Kind regards,

Bill in Tech Support
(206) 555-1212
Office hours: 6:00 a.m. to 10:00 p.m. Pacific time, Monday-Friday
support@company.example
For a variety of easy-to-use "How-To" guides, please visit support.company.example

Figure 10 The bottom half of a good email response

97

Communicating via Texting

(txtng: a gr8 way 2 communic8…maybe)

Know who is on the other end

Some people are very good at texting and others are not. For some people, texting is very natural and comfortable, for others texting is one of the most unnatural and uncomfortable acts of modern times. Texting can be a very efficient method of communication when done between two people who are both proficient. When one person is uncomfortable with it, however, it can hinder communication or, at worst, prevent any communication from happening.

Text transmissions are not 100% reliable

Another consideration in texting is the technical reliability of the process. Because the successful transmission of text messages is dependent upon cellular carriers networks, the sending and receiving of of text message transmissions is not 100% reliable. Most of us have, at some point, sent text messages that weren't received until hours or even days later.

Texting can be expensive

Some people don't include text messaging in their cell phone plans. For them, texting can get very expensive very quickly. Obviously, you should avoid sending them text messages and use email or voice calls instead.

Texting is great for short messages

The technical term for texting is SMS or Short Message Service. It's great for quick messages, but not for involved conversations.

Good uses of texting

- To let an end-user know you're on your way
- To let your user know you're delayed and your approximate time of arrival
- To set up a meeting time
- To check on availability for a phone call
- To set a meeting place
- To ask quick questions requiring no answer or only a short answer
- To send a quick update (for example, "The server is going down for maintenance at midnight.")

Bad uses of texting

- When driving or doing other things that require your attention
- When in a meeting or social gathering with other people (it's just rude)
- When the other person is uncomfortable with it or doesn't include it in his/her cell plan
- Lengthy conversations
- Anything requiring a lot of typing

Be careful about the use of abbreviations, especially those for which the definition is inappropriate for the workplace. If the abbreviation stands for words that are usually considered profane, don't use it in text messages related to work.

Communicating via Instant Messaging (IM)

Instant messaging (or chat) is frequently used for customer support. It offers many benefits including the ability to send the end user a transcript of the support session.

The rules for polite conversation also apply to IM conversations:

- Introduce yourself and include your contact information at the beginning of the session
- As with texting, think short. Although IM is more conducive to long conversations than texting, briefer is still better. If what you need to say won't fit in the chat window without scrolling, consider using email instead.
- Be careful what you write. As with email, anything you say in a chat session can be saved and circulated.
- Give the other person time to respond. Some people type slower than others. Sometimes distractions prevent an immediate response. Remember that conversations are a give and take process. Let the other person respond before you send additional messages.
- Keep it light and professional. Chat sessions are not the place to criticize a user (or anyone else, for that matter). They are great for walking users step-by-step through a procedure, for sending out quick informational updates, and for answering user questions.
- Be careful about using common chat and texting abbreviations. While you might think BRB or LOL are universally known,

they are not. In the same way that you would avoid slang and jargon during in-person encounters, the same idea applies in chat sessions.

- Since chat sessions are emotionless, it can be desirable to use emoticons (such as an occasional smiley face) during chat sessions.

- Write your chat messages in a professional manner. It is easy to get in a hurry and rush through sessions, especially during a hectic workday. Be careful, however, about spelling and grammar in chat. Poor spelling and grammar can actually change the meaning of what is being said, sometimes with unintended consequences.

- If you often receive support requests via chat, be sure to use an away message when you have stepped away from your desk. Consider including in the message your anticipated time of return.

Chapter Eight:
How to Say "No" without Alienating Your End User

"Good judgment comes
from experience, and
experience--well that
comes from poor
judgment."

–Aesop

Sometimes, what the end-user wants simply can't be done. When that happens, the skillful desktop support staffer delivers the news in a way that is clear, yet non-offensive. Alternatives, when available, may be offered, but the key lies in finding a way to say no without leaving the end-user feeling neglected or ignored.

- The art of no
- Dealing with the unsolvable problem
- Getting end-user buy-in
- What to do when you don't know or can't find the answer

The Customer Service Challenge

When your job is to support end-users, it is hard to say "no" to some end-user requests that come your way. Customer service is all about helping people and solving problems, and, from the user's perspective, that implies that you will go out of your way to accept any and all requests. A primary role of IT support is to serve and support end-users, and that involves solving problems and filling needs as requested. But you have to serve more than just individual end-user needs – you also have to serve company interests, professional ethics, and technology best practices. Users may believe they would have an easier time of it if they could ignore security measures and do away with user IDs and passwords, but doing so would not be in the best interest of the organization. Sometimes, workplace interests or policies must take priority over end-user interests, and you may need to say "no", even if you are technically capable of fulfilling the request.

When to Say "No" to an End-User?

Not all issues that require a "no" answer are security-related. There are other things to consider and questions you should ask yourself before you agree to help an end-user when the request is not common and ordinary. For example:

- Do you have the time to complete the request? You may have a genuine desire and willingness to help fulfill a special request, but not enough time.

- Does your schedule allow you to spend time on a custom solution for one user?

- Do you have the resources to complete the request? You may be inundated with requests that have a higher priority, and cannot ask for help to fulfill the request right now. In this case, you may have to say "no".

- Are you qualified to complete the request? You may have a genuine desire to help, and would like to learn more about a certain tool or technique, but

- Do you really have the skills to work on this issue?

- Do you have the authority to fulfill this request? You may have been given instructions not to take on certain types of requests. Sometimes end-users can ask you to go above and beyond what your policies and procedures recommend.

- Are you really authorized to abandon the policies that are in place?

- What might the consequences be if you do?

- Is the request within the scope of your responsibilities?

Giving yourself an honest answer to these questions sometimes leads you to the conclusion that you must say "no". Regardless of how much you want to help the end-user or how skilled you are, you cannot follow through with it for one reason or another. When you must refuse an end-user request, you want to do so without an outright "no" response. If you are abrupt or alienate your end-users, they may bypass you in the future, complain about you, or just go over your head. So the art here is to say "no" without actually using the word. This can be accomplished carefully, but not unless you have thoroughly examined all of the factors that may affect your decision to reject the request.

Considerations before Saying "No"

Consider who is making the service request

Before you turn down a service request, you need to consider "who is asking?" Because of someone's rank or political status in the organization, you may not be able to say " no", even if "no" is the right answer. Think twice before saying "yes" in these circumstances, though, because you should not promise to handle an issue on which you can't follow through. Sometimes you need to get more information or talk to your manager or get advice before providing an answer to someone. You only have so many hours in the day, and saying "yes" without thinking it over carefully or consulting with your coworkers or management team may stop you from fulfilling other tasks that are required to do your job adequately.

Listen and make sure you fully understand the request

In order to respond to a request properly, you need to make sure you understand the nature and scope of the request, and how it relates to projects already underway, new projects, or workplace initiatives. Let your end-users talk, and show them that you are listening by making the appropriate responses, such as suggesting how to solve the problem. If you turn down the request without fully understanding it, you may regret it later, and cause your end-user to be frustrated.

Evaluate the request

Evaluate the request in order to determine whether you can and should or are required to say "yes", or decide to turn down the request. In your deliberations, you need to consider company policies, priorities you have been given, your schedule, resources, skills and other related issues.

Craft your answer

Considering the type of request information you discovered during your evaluation, you will develop a response that fits into one of the following categories:

- "Yes" you agree to fulfill the request

- "No" with an explanation; you can't complete the request and reasons why

- An alternative or compromise

- A referral to the name of someone else that is authorized, or has the skills or time to fulfill the request.

In cases where you must refuse the request, you need to explain your decision. By taking the time to offer an explanation, the reasons for turning down the request take priority over the rejection itself. This gives you a chance to explain your decision. Giving an explanation could help you later if someone complains about your response. If you just say "no" without an explanation, it would be harder to justify and defend your decision. Your role as a support person is to serve the organization and your end-users. If others perceive that you are not serving your users and are refusing requests without just reasons, you may not be in your position for very long.

Offer your explanation

How you choose to communicate your response will depend on several factors: the nature of the request (formal or informal), the person making the request, your relationship with that person, the sensitivity of your response, and the culture of your workplace. You may choose to make your response in person, on the phone, through e-mail, or a combination of methods. No matter which method you choose, you should always follow a few basic techniques:

- **Don't be defensive or apologetic.** Simply state that you regret that you cannot complete the request at this time, and offer your explanation (time conflicts, conflicts with internal policies, conflicts with other plans or projects, security reasons). Emphasize the reason, not the fact you are turning down the request. Using the word "because" in your response helps the end-user receive your message. Using the word "because" gives a logical framework to what you are saying, and helps the person receiving the message accept your logic. "I can't help you to create a new login for a temporary worker because it is against security policies." (If the user pushes you on issues such as this, you can always offer to escalate the issue to your supervisor.)

- **Be as positive as possible.** Focus on any compromise or alternative that you can offer. Always leave yourself an opening for a graceful exit. Your end-user may offer an alternative of their own, tell you what they think is wrong with your logic, or react negatively to your response. If necessary, leave yourself a way to "re-think" the matter so that you can seek assistance from your own management. Try a simple statement such as "if you have any questions, or feel that I have misunderstood your request in any way, please let me know". Let the end-user know that you are still open to seeking a workable solution.

Be Proactive

Having to turn down an end-user's request can be difficult and stressful. You need the right combination of communication and interpersonal skills to carry it off. You can take proactive steps to make the process easier.

- Seek advice and guidance from your manager when necessary. At the very least, it is wise to notify your manager if a problem is likely to occur with an unhappy user, or if the user will be contacting the manager. (You never want your manager to be blindsided by an upset end user. If you know a user is going to contact your manager, it is always best that the manager get a "heads-up" from you.) Also, when you have to make a difficult decision, you should be able to ask for advice or help as needed.

- Set structured procedures and formats to use when you submit responses to end-user requests. If you establish and enforce a structured process, which may include filling out a form or issuing a ticket number for end-user requests, you will minimize the familiarity associated by being able to ask for special favors or informal demands that you may forget or be unable to follow through on. Using a structured request process will improve your IT support services

- Organize yourself, your schedule, and prioritize your workload for efficiency.

Instead of turning users down with the word "no", find another way to say it

You are required to serve your users, and it is never easy to say "no". Your challenge is to balance the need to serve multiple end-users, with the need to meet overall priorities and serve workplace interests. Sometimes a "no" is necessary to meet that goal, but it is often not necessary to use that word.

Avoiding the Word "No"

After you have decided that you will not be able to fulfill an end-users request, develop a better way to refuse the request that the user will be able to accept than the word "no." This may take a little research, and you should develop a list of solutions and alternatives. For example, rather than saying "no", say that you will work on their problem and you will find a suitable solution. You can also say something like, "We are unable to provide that service," but don't say "no". The word "no" gives rise to too many emotional issues, and can put people off.

Some people will ask too much, and at some point you have to cut them off, but do it without saying "no". In addition, point out all that you have given and all that you have attempted to do to right their problem. Help them to accept that they have been taken care of, and that you have exhausted all options to solve their problem. Think about how you like to be treated when you call in for support, and then deliver that same consideration to your end-user. It's how you say "no" that matters.

You can't accommodate everyone, so find or create alternatives. Brainstorm difficult end-user service problems with your team. Share each new alternative solution that you come up with that can be used over and over again. Document these solutions. A co-worker may have a smooth way of handling something that puzzles you.

Dealing with Difficult End-Users

There are actually very few genuinely difficult users in the world. You probably think, "You don't know the users in my workplace." However, the majority of users in the world are reasonable people. They may not think the way, look the way, or sound the way that you do. However, they are your users, and it is your job to deal with them. They may get "difficult" from time to time if they feel they've been let down. It's how you handle them that will determine if they continue to be a problem, or if you can turn them around.

Difficult situations and angry users usually occur because some part of our core service has failed, or the user perceives it to have failed. We have not delivered on time, the user has the wrong product, it doesn't work, or it's not what the user expected. What happens next is that the user comes to the interaction with us in a negative or angry frame of mind. It's what happens next that will decide whether they deal with you again or complain about you to other people. Remember, anger is a natural, self-defensive reaction to a perceived wrong. If there is a problem with your company's product or service, some frustration and disappointment is justified.

The trick is not just to concentrate on fixing the core service issues. Telling the user that you'll replace the product, deliver it in half an hour, or change the system so the problem will never happen again, may not be possible. It does not help to give them this answer if you cannot fulfill it. Sometimes you may not have an answer, and the end-user is going to hear "no".

Why Some Situations Go Wrong

You don't care

You don't sound or act as if you care, are concerned or appreciate the end-user's situation. Maybe you do care, but in order to convey your caring, you've got to say caring words and sound compassionate, as if you care. Nobody can read your mind. You might try to say things like "I know this is very frustrating." "I'm sure I would feel the same way if I were you." "I am so very sorry." "If there was anything at all that I could do, believe me, I would." It's amazing how much of a calming effect that can have.

You don't listen

Too often we try to jump in with solutions, and don't allow the end-users to vent their feelings. You need to show the end-user that you're listening by what you say, and how you say it. Understand that obnoxious users are often embarrassed because they made a mistake and want to blame it on you. Showing that you are interested in what they have to say often helps you to create good relations with the user. Active listening techniques, including asking to make sure you understand what they have said can go a long way toward fostering a good situation. By saying, "Let me make sure I understand what you said." you are reaching out to the user and showing you care.

111

You let the user upset you

It is easy to allow the user's attitude to irritate or annoy you. The user picks up on this through your tone of voice and use of language, or your silence, and this fans the fire. Make it a game or challenge to see how many upset users you can turn around. Don't take upset users' ranting and raving personally. Don't get emotionally hooked. When you let users "push your buttons", you lose. When you respond emotionally-with anger, sarcasm, or blame, you can't respond rationally. When things heat up, cool off by saying that you need to research the situation and possible solutions, and ask if you may get back to them at a later time.

You use the wrong words

Some trigger words cause users to become more difficult. Some of these are "can't, have to, sorry about that". Be sure to offer users an alternative. Choices provide users some say in how they want to proceed. Instead of saying "I don't know," try "Let me get you an answer," or "Let me find out for you."

You focus on yourself instead of seeing it from the user's point of view

Maybe you think the end-user is making too much out of a small issue. It is human nature to love being RIGHT, knowing that the other person is WRONG for asking for whatever it is that they are asking for. And sometimes we think that if we show compassion for their situation, we are telling them that they are RIGHT for asking. You think to yourself, "What's the big deal? I'll fix it right away". No matter what, it IS a big deal for the user, and they want you to acknowledge that.

End-users will often judge the level of your service based on how well you recover from a difficult situation and they are very likely to forgive you when you do it well. Difficult situations or "screw-ups" are opportunities to win supporters for life. Everybody makes mistakes. The ways we deal with our mistakes communicates who we really are.

If your actions show people that you truly care about them and their needs, and that you dislike having to say "no" to their request, you both win! They will walk away knowing that even though you had to decline their request, you tried everything in your power to give them what they wanted. They will appreciate you, and will show you courtesy in return.

Interactive Exercise: Working Magic with End-Users

This exercise is best done with a group of three or four, but you can certainly do it by yourself.

If you're in a group...

Work through these scenarios together. Start by reading about the situation.

If you're working by yourself...

Read through the scenario, then on a separate sheet of paper, write down your solution. It is often helpful to write down your solution one day, then re-visit your solution a day or two later and see if you would change anything.

Whether you're in a group or by yourself, decide how you would approach the end-user, and then write a script for what you would say to handle the situation.

Use your best communication skills to provide an answer for the end-user.

1. A manager of the Sales Department calls and wants a contractor he has hired to have access to the network. He is asking you for a special favor, even though it is company policy that only employees can have network access.

2. An end-user calls to complain that when he walks away from his desk to attend meetings in the conference room his access times out, and he has to log in up to five times a day. He is frustrated, and wants you to change the timing on his computer to avoid being logged out of the system. You cannot reset the timing. This is a regulatory and a security policy.

3. A project manager in a work group wants to set up a local share with her team. She is calling you to create permission for her to do this. You know that it is against company policy to set up permission for a local share.

4. It is company policy that no one can download and install software. A graphic designer has been waiting for six weeks to get InDesign, required for her project, which is due next week. Her manager has approved the purchase order, but the software has not arrived. She wants to be able to download the trial version over the Internet to meet her deadline.

5. A software developer is putting together a project proposal for acquiring enterprise-wide software. He needs your help to investigate how this software will work with remote users on three different platforms. Your schedule is full, and your manager has just given you three tasks that you need to accomplish by Friday.

6. A user complains that her computer is running slowly. Upon investigation, you find that she has many programs open at the same time.

7. A department head wants you to take a look at his personal laptop because it's been running slowly.

8. An upper-level executive wants you to help her add a stock ticker, streaming music, or Skype to her computer. Such programs can adversely affect network performance and are not permitted by policy.

Chapter Nine:
Stress Management

> "Write your injuries in dust, your benefits in marble."
>
> --Benjamin Franklin

Let's face it: End-User desktop support can be one of the most stressful positions in all of IT because you face the same problems every day from different callers. In this session, you'll learn practical, down-to-earth techniques for dealing positively with the inevitable stress of a desktop support position.

- The impact of stress

- The stress management equation

- What's in your control – and what's not

- Personal stress activators

- You can influence the stress outcome

Managing Your Stress

Stress is the body's non-specific response to any demands made on it. It is the way our bodies react to our continually changing environment. Stress has physical and emotional effects on us, and can create positive or negative feelings. The important thing to remember about stress is that certain forms of stress are normal and essential.

Why Some Stress Is Good For You

Many of us think of stress as a synonym for tension or pressure. Actually, stress is just the way we respond to change. Understanding stress and its effects can help you use it to your own advantage, and turn potential "stressors" into positive challenges.

Good Stress

Stress can be good when it helps us perform better. Certain forms and levels of stress keep us alert and productive. Stress can help us finish that paper that is due, complete the race when our resources are depleted, or answer a record number of support calls in a shift.

"Good stress", also called eustress, arises from situations and events that we think of as positive, but which still trigger the stress response. These can include getting a promotion, graduating, starting a new job, moving, making more money, getting married, and even going on vacation. These good things are stressful because they involve a change in the way we act or think about things. Change is stressful, whether or not we label it as good or bad.

Bad Stress

Stress is bad (distress) when it causes us to be upset or makes us sick. Bad stress causes negative feelings, health problems, and lowers productivity. Once you have begun to experience the effects or symptoms of bad stress, you have gone beyond your optimal stress level.

Problems that arise that are beyond our control can and often do result in bad stress. Examples are a teen taking the family car for a spin, a baby spiking a fever in the middle of the night, layoffs at work, or an unexpected dental bill.

Intensity vs. Duration

Understanding your stress level is important. If nothing in your life causes you any stress or excitement, you may become bored, depressed, or may not be living up to your potential. If everything in your life, or large portions of your life, cause you stress, you may experience health or mental problems that will make your behavior worse.

Recognizing when you are stressed and managing your stress can greatly improve your life. Some short-term stress -- for example what you feel before an important job interview, test, presentation, or sporting event -- may give you the extra energy you need to perform at your best. But long-term stress -- for example constant worry over your job, school, money, or family -- may actually drain your energy and deplete your ability to perform well.

Short-term stress occurs when you find yourself under pressure in a particular situation. Short-term high intensity-stress helps you feel alert and alive. The rush of adrenalin helps you focus on the situation at hand. If you have had a "near-miss" while driving a car you have likely experienced short-term high-intensity stress. We recover from this type of stress fairly quickly, and rarely does it cause lasting problems. This kind of stress can be your ally.

Distress (Usually Bad)	Eustress (Usually Good)
Often Low-intensity/High-duration	Often High-intensity/Low-duration

Distress stress comes from a buildup of stress over a long period. Sustained levels of even moderate stress can lead to serious physical and mental illness if not controlled. Most of us are dealing with moderate level, day-after-day stress and this is the kind that grinds us up and spits us out. Managing distress begins with understanding a simple formula.

Stress Management Equation

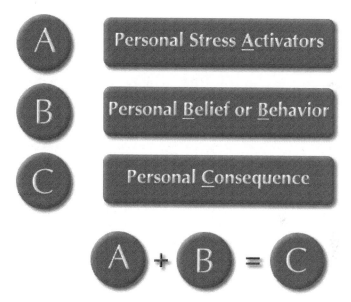

Figure 11 The stress management equation

For example, let's say that one of your stress activators is conflict. Your personal belief is to confront conflict aggressively. Suppose that you have a conflict (A) with your boss. Because your personal belief (B) is to stand up for yourself and your personal behavior (B) is to confront conflict aggressively, you stand up to your boss, tell her that she's an idiot, and slam the door as you storm out of the office. Your personal consequence (C) could well be that you'll lose your job.

121

Consider this alternative: You have a conflict (A) with your boss. After losing your last job because of your personal behavior (B) to confront conflict aggressively, you decided to keep your personal belief (B) to stand up for yourself, but to modify your personal behavior (B) by respectfully saying to your boss that you disagree with her and asking her to help you understand her position. Your personal consequence now could be to win the respect of your boss and keep your job.

Physical and Mental Signs of Stress

You've heard before that recognizing when you are under stress is the first step in learning how to deal with your stress, but what does that mean? Sometimes we are so used to living with stress that we don't know how to identify it.

Whether you are experiencing immediate or short-term stress or have been experiencing stress for a long time or long-term stress, your body and mind may be showing the effects. The following table shows some examples of stress activators. You probably have some of your own that may be different from those in the table.

This table shows some of the things that can cause stress (stress activators):

Stress Activators
Conflict
Impossible deadlines
Regulatory environment
Ambiguity
Disorganization
Water cooler politics
Change
Lack of resources

This table shows some beliefs that people have:

Personal Belief Set A	Personal Belief Set B
It's a black and white world	The world is comprised of varying shades of gray.
You're either with me or against me	You and I may not agree on everything. We both understand that there are often several correct paths to a destination.
You've got to stand your ground no matter what	As we receive new information, sometimes a course correction is necessary.
Other people need to understand where I'm coming from	Remember Stephen Covey's wisdom, "Seek first to understand, then to be understood."

This table shows some behaviors that people use:

Personal Behavior Set A	Personal Behavior Set B
Get in your face and tell you what I think.	Respectfully say I disagree with you and ask you to help me understand your position.
Work long hours without saying anything and think of yourself as a martyr.	Document your hours, discuss the workload with your boss, and ask how best to deal with the problem.
Gossip about the boss and your co-workers, spread the latest rumors you hear.	Inform yourself as to the facts of the various issues facing your organization, stop spreading gossip and innuendo.
Agree to everything, but do nothing (passive aggressive behavior).	Meet with your boss or co-worker, respectfully and professionally explain the issue(s) you have with what you have been asked to do, and ask for help in finding ways to resolve those issues.
When faced with a lack of necessary resources, make arbitrary decisions about where to cut corners, disregarding the effect on quality.	Ask your boss for help in deciding what to cut due to the lack of resources.

After reviewing the two sets of beliefs and behaviors, think about which sets of beliefs and which set of behaviors will most likely have a positive outcome for all parties involved, have a positive effect on your career, and most likely gain you the most respect from your boss and co-workers.

If you identified personal belief and behavior set B as the set most likely to produce a positive outcome, you're well on your way to personal happiness and career success. If you identified personal belief and behavior set A the best way of thinking about things and dealing with stress, you may want to re-think your paths to personal happiness and career success.

Keep your mind open to new ways of looking at things and new ways of reacting to the things that happen to you. Bear in mind that just because something is new doesn't mean it is better and just because something is old does not mean it is better. Similarly, just because something is new does not mean it is bad, nor just because something is old does not mean it is bad.

> "Fifteen hundred years ago everybody knew the Earth was the center of the universe. Five hundred years ago, everybody knew the Earth was flat, and fifteen minutes ago, you knew that humans were alone on this planet. Imagine what you'll know tomorrow." --Agent K in Men in Black

This table shows some common warning signs that stress may be affecting your body and mind:

Stress Warning Signals
Tiredness
Feeling on edge
Anxiety
Depression
Long-term health condition
Boredom
Insomnia

If you're experiencing any of these signals, something is not right in your life. Whether it is stress or something else, the above signals are warning signs telling you that something is wrong. Whether you deal with it personally or by seeking help, it is important to deal with it early. Untreated, stress can lead to serious health problems.

Personal Exercise: Dealing Positively with Your Stress

On the next page is a table to help you identify your sources of stress. The table will also help you identify whether you can control those sources or not.

Make a list in the area marked *source* of what causes you stress. Include work-related issues and non-work related issues. Check the appropriate box to indicate whether the stress is high-intensity/low-duration or low-intensity/high-duration. (We are more concerned with low-intensity/high-duration stress.) Finally, in the area marked *solution,* jot down something you can do to positively deal with the source of the stress. Often, we can deal positively with stress by simply recognizing its source and choosing a different response from past responses.

It is very important to recognize that there are some sources of stress that we can't control. When we have no control over a source of stress, our best choice is to simply let it go.

The Serenity Prayer

God grant me the serenity
to accept the things I cannot change;
courage to change the things I can;
and wisdom to know the difference.

For example, if you are stuck in a traffic jam with no way out, as frustrating and as maddening as it seems, there's nothing you can do about it. You can choose your reaction and, regardless of whether you choose to get angry and upset or to simply accept it and listen to your favorite music on the radio, you'll still get to your destination at the same time. If you choose to get angry and upset, you'll introduce more stress into your life, potentially causing stress-induced illness or other negative outcomes. If you choose to accept that you cannot change the current situation, you can also choose to create a calm, serene experience for yourself as you wait for the traffic to clear. Your reaction is completely your choice.

	Source of Stress and Solution	High-Intensity, Low-Duration	Low-Intensity High-Duration
1.	Source	❑	❑
	Solution		
2.	Source	❑	❑
	Solution		
3.	Source	❑	❑
	Solution		
4.	Source	❑	❑
	Solution		
5.	Source	❑	❑
	Solution		
6.	Source	❑	❑
	Solution		

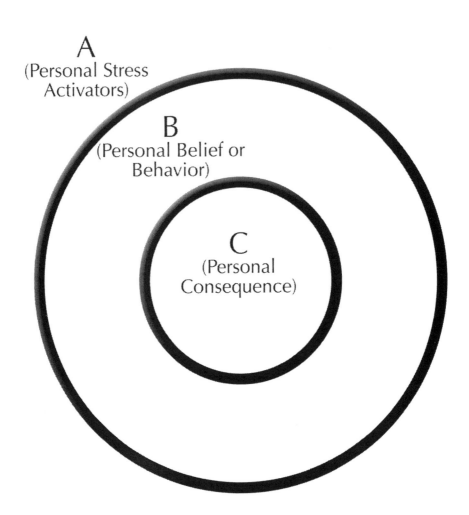

Figure 12 Personal stress management tool

Personal Stress Management Tool

Step One: Around the outer circle (A), write the things that cause you stress.

Step Two: Make a copy of the page with all of your stress activators and set it aside for a moment.

Step Three: Back on the original page, in the next circle (B), write beliefs or behaviors that you use to deal with the stress. In the bullseye (C), write the personal consequence(s) of your beliefs or behaviors.

Step Four: Now, on the copy of the page, start in the bullseye (C) and write the desired personal consequences or outcomes (what you would like to have happen ideally). Next, write new beliefs or behaviors that you could use to deal appropriately with the stress.

Yes, I'm Stressed – Now What?!

Everyone has the freedom to choose his/her response to any situation. Freedom to choose is a condition of the mind; liberty is a condition of the environment. How many of these items that you listed do you have some control or choice over?

You can choose to be proactive, and work at approaching stressors with a different attitude. You can try to accept those things that at the present you can't control, while focusing your efforts on the things that you can change. Change your vocabulary from "If I only had" to "I can be…" Focus on changing from the inside-out. Try using a different approach, and by being different, to effect a more positive change in what's outside of yourself.

Dealing with Stress

One of the most immediate and easiest ways to deal with stress is responding to your body's physical symptoms. Sometimes this can be as easy as stopping what you're doing and taking a few deep, relaxing breaths.

- *Are irate callers getting on your nerves?* Go into another room, or even the bathroom or closet if you need to get away! Shut the door. Experience the quiet. Take a few deep breaths. Feel the tension go out of your head, neck and shoulders.
- *Have you had another bad day with your boss or co-worker?* Walk down the hall, rinse your face in cool water in the bathroom, or head outside and walk around the block. Just getting away for a few minutes can be calming and help you relax.
- *Have you spent too long sitting at your computer?* Push back from your desk. Roll your head and shoulders. Rub your hands together quickly to warm them and place them over your weary eyes, or just close your eyes and let your face and neck relax. Breathe in and out slowly and deeply.

- *Do you need a shoulder to cry on?* Do you have someone you can talk to about what's happening in your life? Having someone you can share both the good and bad with is important.
- *Laugh.* Nothing relieves the tension in your body, or your mind, like a good laugh. Go find a funny video on YouTube.
- *Find a Distraction.* Join a group or organization where people share your interests. Take up a new hobby.
- *Are you too focused on your problems?* Get outside of your own problems. There are bigger issues in the world. Choose an issue that you care about and donate time and energy working to overcome it. When you are busy helping others, your problems seems smaller.

Whether you start to take yoga classes, decide to organize your finances, or go to a comedy club with a friend to help you deal with stress, you have options. Stress can seem overwhelming. Stress can be isolating. But you are not alone; and you can minimize stress, and make it work for you.

The Importance of Breathing

No matter how you choose to deal with your stress, it is important to understand the power of controlled breathing. Normally, we breathe in short, shallow breaths. When you find yourself in a stressful situation or when you simply want to relax for a moment, try controlled breathing. Sit on the edge of your chair, back straight, with your hands in your lap or resting on your knees. Close your eyes, if you wish. Breathe in through your nose to a count of five and exhale through your nose to a count of five. Repeat five times (or more, if you like).

soundtraining.net
accelerated i.t. training

Get Out of Stress Free Card

Make a copy of this page and pin it to your wall or keep it in an easily accessible place. Jot down things that make you feel peaceful and happy. You can also paste small pictures of people, places, and things that make you feel peaceful and happy. When you find yourself feeling stress, take a minute and look at this card.

Appendix:
Six Articles on Customer Service

The following articles were written by Don R. Crawley. They are based on the preceding text.

Note from the author:

The following articles are blog posts written mainly in 2007. I translated much of the material in the blog posts into sections in the book, but I wanted to include the original posts because of their more personal style of writing and as reinforcement for things you read earlier in the book.

Today, I blog at:

- www.soundtraining.net/blog
- www.compassionategeek.com

Ten Ways to Delight Your End User

By Don R. Crawley

As an IT support technician, you could very well be a hero to your user today! Your job is incredibly important, because you are often the bridge between where a user is on a project and where s/he wants to be. You even have the power to help your users have a great day by solving their problems and freeing them to think more creatively and be more productive in their jobs. There are many studies that have shown how well-trained IT support personnel add directly to a company's bottom line by helping employees work more productively and creatively. Here are ten simple and practical techniques you can put to use today to start making a positive difference in peoples' lives.

Respond quickly

Quick responses can take several forms. Ideally, you simply answer the phone and solve the problem. Anyone who has spent any time in an IT support position knows that's not always possible, so what other options exist? Automated voice response systems that let callers know about how long they should expect to wait are great; email responses that do the same thing are also great. The key is to inform users as to the approximate wait time until they get a response. Armed with accurate information, users can then make an informed decision as to whether to wait on hold or hang up and call back later. If they're communicating via email, they can make a decision about whether to wait for a response or move on to another project and return to the one requiring support at a later time.

First impressions count

Start the call or in-person visit with a pleasant, professional greeting and for heaven's sake, be real! In other words, a simple,

"Hello, this is Don Crawley. May I help you?" is far better than some contrived greeting such as, "Hello, this is Don Crawley. How may I provide excellent service to you today?" (If your organization requires you to say specific words in your greeting, work on making them genuine. Nothing is worse than hearing someone answer the phone reading a script in a monotone voice or a condescending tone. When you're forced to use a standardized greeting, try to understand your employer's intent in requiring the standardized greeting. Even if you think the words you're required to say are phony, your employer's intent is not phony; your employer wants you to deliver excellent service, so find a way to believe it and mean it when you say it. Make it real!)

Display honest competence

Tell callers that you'll either fix their problem, find someone who can, or find a workaround. No one has all the answers and no one expects you to have all the answers. They do, however, expect you to be familiar with common troubleshooting techniques, to be honest about your abilities, and to be honest when you don't know the answer.

Reassure

Reassure your users that you're committed to solving their problems. Saying things like, "Tracy, I'm creating a file on this issue so I can follow up on it and make sure we solve it for you", assures your user that you're taking ownership of their problem. In fact, when you say those exact words, "I'm taking ownership of this issue", you tell your users that you're with them and you're going to see the issue through to some sort of resolution, whether it's actually solving the problem, escalating it, or developing a work-around.

Keep it positive

Focus on what you WILL do instead of what you WON'T do.
Keep the conversation upbeat, even when the user wants to
complain about things unrelated to the problem at hand. Your user
doesn't want to hear you complain about computers, Microsoft, the
company, or any of the myriad things people complain about.
Dare to be different and avoid the temptation to join users in their
complaining.

Empathize

Empathize with your user. You can empathize without
complaining. Use empathetic statements like, "I don't blame you.
I'd be frustrated too, if that happened to me." Ross Shafer says
people don't want customer *service* as much as they want customer
empathy. Imagine how you'd feel if you were under deadline and
a document failed to print. Imagine how you'd feel if you were
trying to get out the door and your computer locked up.
Remember the three "S's": Keep it sincere, short, and then deliver
a solution (or at least a workaround).

Be gracious

Similar to empathy, graciousness helps endear you to users; it lets
users know you appreciate them and what they're going through in
trying to do their job. As you're working on their problems, thank
them for calling and let them know how much you appreciate the
opportunity to help. (The reality is that, when they call and ask us
to help, we can often head off bigger problems down the road. We
really DO appreciate the opportunity, because it can save us a lot
of time and frustration in the future!) As always, be careful to be
sincere. People can easily detect insincerity.

Be respectful

Thanks to the mass media, our society has become disrespectful. It's not necessary to respect someone in order to treat them respectfully. In the movie, "The Green Mile", Tom Hanks' character treats condemned criminals on death row with respect. Certainly, persuasive arguments can be made that the condemned men with whom he dealt were not deserving of respect, but he treated them respectfully anyway. People tend to behave the way you expect them to. Often, the way you're treated is a mirror of how you treat others.

Offer one bonus tip

This could be something new that you've discovered in a widely-used application such as Microsoft Outlook or a new resource available on the company's network. Use good judgment on this; if your user is obviously in a hurry to get back to work, save your bonus tip for later. If, on the other hand, you've established rapport with your user, offer a bonus tip by saying something like, "By the way, Pat, we're letting everyone know about a way to color code appointments in Outlook. It's really easy and people seem to use it a lot once they know about it. Are you aware of this?"

Remember, the final three questions

"Have I solved your problem?", "Are you satisfied with the way I handled this incident?", and "Is there anything I could have done better?" I often recommend starting the session by telling the user that you'll be asking those three questions at the end of the session.

As with all things, be sensitive to your users' mood and circumstance. If they're obviously in a hurry or angry, avoid small talk and say something like, "I can tell you're in a hurry, so I'm going to be respectful of your time and just get to work on your problem." or, "I can tell you're upset right now. I don't blame you at all, so I'm going to get right to work on solving this issue." Be sure to punctuate lengthy periods of silence with comments like, "I'm not ignoring you; I'm still working on this problem." If the person with whom you're dealing is technically sophisticated, you could even let him/her know what you're doing. If, on the other hand, the user is not technically sophisticated, just let him/her know you're not ignoring them.

Above all, remember that our jobs in Information Systems and Technology are not about technology at all; they're about delivering creative solutions to workplace problems. Everything revolves around our users. We have to help them be more productive and creative in their jobs by helping them be more proficient with the tools of Information Systems and Technology.

A High Level of Professionalism

By Don R. Crawley

Professionalism means that how you speak and act and the emails or other materials you send reflect a high level of training and expertise. This becomes the professional image that you project to your users. Here are some ways you can project a professional image to users on the phone:

Smile

A smile on your face affects how your voice sounds on the phone. Smiling creates more pleasant resonance in a phone voice and is the first step in conveying a professional image. Maybe you've heard the phrase, "Smile and dial!" Some professionals who use the phone place mirrors at their desks so they can check their smile before talking on the phone.

Keep it Positive

We know how a positive attitude is self-fulfilling. Your users deserve a cheerful approach on every interaction. IT support personnel must perform extreme self-care in order to approach each phone call positively. If you feel you cannot be positive on the next phone call, ask your manager for a few minutes to take a walk or get a bite to eat. Your users will be grateful that you took a break so you can return with a fresh attitude.

Speak Clearly

Mumbling conveys a lack of confidence. Enunciating and speaking in a clear, moderate tone of voice conveys confidence and professionalism. Listen carefully to yourself speak and you will be amazed how much better your annunciation becomes. You will also pay more attention to the words you use.

Develop Rapport

Being "in rapport" means being in sync with your user's communication style. Have you ever instantly liked someone you were talking to over the phone, even though you had not met them and do not know them personally? Chances are that you were in rapport with them. They may have been using some techniques that are very effective to make you feel at home with them.

Mirroring is a subtle way to conform your behavior to match the behavior of your user. It is the genuine search for areas of similarity between you and your communication partner, and its purpose is to make people feel comfortable with you. There are several auditory ways to create rapport through mirroring on the phone:

- Matching your rate of speech and the tone of your voice to that of your user

- Using the same verbal expressions and repeating or paraphrasing what your user has said

If the user is speaking slowly and you normally speak very quickly, moderate your normal rate of speech. If your user is using a loud voice, speak up just a bit. Remember, you do not want to mirror the aggressive behavior or anger of a user. If the user uses an incorrect technical term, use the same language at first and then gently educate the user by saying "We also call that the file extension."

Repeating or paraphrasing is an excellent way to mirror the user's communication style. It is also a powerful listening technique. A good time to use paraphrasing is when you are asking a series of questions while troubleshooting. You can repeat or paraphrase a few key words of the user's answer to confirm your understanding.

Avoid slang, colloquialisms, profanity and terms of endearment

People from other parts of the country or the world may not understand some of the terms you may use when speaking casually to your friends. IT support personnel should always use professional language in speaking to users. Professional language does not include profanity, terms of endearment such as "honey," "sweetie," "buddy," or "pal," or slang. An exception to this rule is when speaking with a user with whom you have a personal relationship, but a wise IT support person will still exercise caution when communicating with any user.

Demonstrating and Maintaining Your Competence

By Don R. Crawley

Competence means providing correct, knowledgeable service, performed with accuracy and confidence. Competence is a two-part process. You must demonstrate competence in the way you do your job, but you must also find ways to maintain your technical competence.

Demonstrating Competence

Here are a couple of good techniques to use to demonstrate your competence:

Tell the user what you are going to do before you do it. This technique is called headlining, in the sense that a newspaper article's headline tells you what you are going to read before you read it. As a user, it is very frustrating to be dealing with a technical support provider who does not tell you what he or she is doing. When there is silence on the phone, the user may be confused, and this does not assure the user of your competence. You know you have not done a good job of headlining if, after a period of silence, your user says, "Are you still there?" The user does not feel cared for if she has to guess if you are still on the line.

Headlining is the mark of a professional IT support provider. It is easy and quick to do, and creates a high degree of end-user satisfaction. Use headlining when you need to take a moment to look up some information in the database. You can say, "It will take me just a minute to look that up in the database." This gives the user the assurance that you are working on their behalf.

Another way of providing assurance to users is to build their confidence in your ability to help them. This can be done with a solution statement delivered once you understand and have confirmed the user's problem. A solution statement simply tells the user that you can help them solve the problem. You can say, "From what you have told me, I know how to solve the problem."

Maintaining Technical Competence

Our world in Information Systems and Technology evolves so quickly that maintaining technical competence can seem overwhelming at times. Here are four keys to maintaining your technical competence:

Be curious.

Curious people are always exploring. When you're curious, life is more interesting and you find new ways of doing things, you find things you didn't even know existed, and you maintain a childlike sense of wonder and awe.

Read...a lot.

The fact that you're reading this article speaks highly of you. It's not that you're reading this particular article (as much as your author wants to believe that!), but that you're reading any article about how to do your job better that speaks so highly of you. There are thousands, perhaps millions, of blogs and forums on the Web dealing with the same technologies you support. Microsoft and most other vendors provide extensive support documentation at their sites. Microsoft even has free hands-on labs and how-to guides. Get one of the O'Reilly Cookbooks for the technology you support and work through recipes that are most interesting to you.

Build a sandbox.

I first heard of an IT "sandbox" when I was working with some individuals from Kimberly-Clark Corporation in a PKI training session. The IT "sandbox" is another name for a testing lab where you can experiment without worrying about system failure. Today, it's often not necessary to set up a physical lab with multiple physical computers. Instead, you can use tools like VMWare, Virtual PC, or VirtualBox to create a virtualized lab environment in which you can test and experiment to your heart's content without worrying about affecting end-users. Some virtualization products are available for free; others at very low cost. (I use VMWare Workstation.) Use Google to learn more about virtualization and the vendors who create virtualization products.

Get trained!

As a training provider to the IT world, you'd certainly expect me to make this recommendation, but it's important. Training, whether in a college classroom, a seminar environment, in a workshop, or at a conference exposes you to new ways of doing things and thinking about things. Electronic delivery of training can be an excellent solution, but participating in in-person classes allows you to interact with the instructor and the other students. It's through such interaction that you discover new concepts and new solutions to old problems. I discovered when I returned to college that just being in an educational environment got me thinking in new and positive ways. Additionally, great teachers and trainers challenge you and help you step outside your comfort zone which is how you affect positive change in your career and in your life.

Being great at your job isn't necessarily easy, but it's immensely rewarding in terms of personal satisfaction, career options, and financial rewards.

How Responsive Are You?

By Don R. Crawley

Responsiveness is the willingness to respond to customer needs by answering their phone or email requests quickly, and being willing to do what it takes to respond effectively to a service request.

Responsiveness is adopting a can-do attitude, and a willingness to go the extra mile for the customer. Recent research studies support the theory that soft skills (such as listening, empathy, courtesy and creating rapport) are more important than technical skills in the career advancement of any employee. This is especially true in the support industry, where most managers have realized that they must hire people who have a good attitude or approach to serving customers plus an aptitude for technical knowledge, and that the rest can be taught.

A positive attitude is the first step in building good soft skills. You have control over your attitude. Just like you can choose what clothes to wear in the morning, you can also choose what attitude to assume every day. You can choose to see the glass as half-full, or half-empty. Your approach, or attitude, toward life is a self-fulfilling prophecy. If your attitude is "Everyone has something to offer me!", then you will interpret everything that happens to you as an interesting journey. On the other hand, if you approach your job and your life in a less than positive way, every bump in the road will seem like a huge obstacle.

Who is that in the mirror?

Several weeks ago, I faced some of the usual challenges of life on the road. Things usually go very well for me and on those rare occasions when things "hiccup", they're usually minor. This week, however, I dealt with a major problem that had the potential to cause a major disruption in my business. Now, as I look back on what happened, I'm beginning to see the entire situation with new clarity. I made several mistakes. The first mistake was in making assumptions about what a vendor would do. I could have spent more time at their website and learned more about their policies and procedures. Instead, I spent a brief time skimming over their services and made assumptions about how to order a particular service and whether it was the right service for me. The second mistake I made was in not contacting this vendor earlier to discuss how best to use their services (and whether they were even the right vendor for this job). The third mistake I made was in trying to deal with this vendor while I was hurrying to catch a train. In other words, I was in a state of stress which undoubtedly came through in my voice (even though I don't think I was rude, demanding, or abusive). As I dealt with this vendor in trying to resolve several problems, I received brusque (almost rude) customer service. I don't believe there is ever a reason to treat any customer in a manner that is anything other than cheerful, pleasant, respectful, and empathetic, but I wonder if there were subtle messages that I was sending that caused me to receive less than exemplary customer service. As I look back at my experiences with other people, I also need to look in the mirror. Am I doing everything I can to have a positive effect on everyone I meet? Have I gone out of my way to touch people in a positive way? When the world doesn't go my way, do I take a moment to stop and regroup or do I complain to everyone around me so they can feel bad, too? I know I can't control other people, but I certainly can control how I appear when they look in my direction.

So, what are the lessons I learned and how do they relate to you as a tech support pro?

Start Early

When you have plenty of time, you're more relaxed and things just seem to go better. Arrive at your desk early. Give yourself 15 or 20 minutes before your shift starts to gather your thoughts and organize your workspace. Then later, when the day starts to get frantic, you'll find you're more in control of things. I knew a football coach who told his players, "If you're not fifteen minutes early, you're late."

Do Enough Research

As a tech support person, do you subscribe to news feeds and blogs about the products you support? Do you spend time each day reading articles and books related to the products you support? Have you set up a virtual lab using VMWare, VirtualPC, or VirtualBox so you can experiment and test your solutions before you offer them to your users? Knowledge is power and the more knowledge you have, the more you'll be empowered to delight your users with relevant, accurate solutions.

Focus

Focus on the task at hand instead of multi-tasking. This means, when your user calls needing help, you focus exclusively on them and nothing else. Even if you think you can multi-task, don't let your users know you're doing it while you're talking to them!

Look in the Mirror

When the world is crashing around you, before you do anything else, look in the mirror. Maybe you can't control the rest of the world, but you are in complete control over how you view the world and what's happening in it.

As a desktop support professional, take a moment to ask yourself the following questions.

1. Do I put myself in the user's shoes?

2. Do I take ownership of a problem and see it through to completion?

3. Am I willing to help both users and co-workers?

4. Do I consciously assume a positive outlook with my users and co-workers?

5. Am I respectful and courteous to the user?

6. Do I treat everyone with respect and courtesy?

7. Do I speak and conduct myself confidently with users?

If you answered yes to at least five, you are on the right track to creating a positive position from which to serve your users for the best results. If you answered yes to fewer than five, your attitude might be keeping you from doing your best to create the proper environment for success in your job.

Make it Dependable and Reliable

By Don R. Crawley

Dependable and reliable service means providing consistently accurate answers and follow-through on your promises. Your end users should consistently get the courteous, pleasant and knowledgeable service every time they contact IT support. Here are three keys to making your service both dependable and reliable.

Under Promise and Over Deliver

To accomplish dependable and reliable service, consider adopting the motto "Under-promise; over-deliver." This familiar guideline reminds you to set expectations with your users at a reasonable level, but one at which you can consistently exceed their expectations. That means giving yourself and your co-workers a cushion when fulfilling promises to users. For example, if you need to research a problem for a user, and you think you can call them back in two hours, discipline yourself to tell the user that you will get back to them in, for example, four hours. This helps you account for those unexpected emergencies that might come up, yet still meet your user's expectations. Some of the airlines are using this technique in establishing their schedules. They know, for example, that under ideal conditions, a particular flight will take two hours. They schedule the flight, however, for two hours and fifteen minutes. That allows them to arrive on time, even when they leave a few minutes late. It's about planning for the unplanned. Using this technique, your users will be wowed, and you will maintain your sanity (and build a great reputation!).

Keep Your Emotions under Control

This means that you don't let things get to you. Your users know that whenever they call, you'll always be level-headed and ready to help solve their problem. Sure, life has its ups and downs, but your users don't need to know about your life's ups and downs. Keep it professional and stay level-headed; let your users grow to expect consistency every time they call. The same concept applies when you're not feeling well or in pain. No one wants to hear about someone else's aches and pains, especially not your users. Put on your game face and wow them with your service. If you're too sick or in too much pain to put on your game face, why are you at work? (And, while we're on the subject, when you're sick with something contagious, stay home. Your colleagues at the office will appreciate you for helping keep the work area healthy and disease free.)

Always Do What You Say You'll Do

When you tell a user that you'll get back to her in 24 hours, get back to her in 24 hours (or less). Sometimes, things don't happen the way you expect: Shipments don't arrive, your sources of information don't get back to you, an office is closed, and so forth. Most people understand that things like that happen; they don't, however, understand that you didn't call them back when you said you would. Even when you don't have new information, call the user back when you say you will or stop by his office when you say you will. The fact that you uphold your word, even on the most seemingly inconsequential things, will speak volumes to your colleagues about your character and the kind of person you are. How you handle the little things tells your bosses, customers, and colleagues how you'll handle the big things. Similar to the concept of under-promise and over-deliver, this is the concept of "promise little; do much".

Dependable and reliable service is about consistency; it's letting your users grow to expect outstanding service every time they request help. Day-in and day-out, you consistently deliver service that delights. If fact, you're so consistent in delighting your users that they take you for granted. And that's a good thing!

What is Your Empathy Quotient?

By Don R. Crawley

How's your empathy quotient? Your ability to empathize may be your most important ability as a member of the IT support staff. Empathy means providing caring and personal service. Dictionary.com defines empathy as "the intellectual identification with...the feelings, thoughts or attitudes of another." Empathy is your ability to truly put yourself in your user's position so you can understand his/her frustration. Once we truly understand our user's frustration, fears, and aggravations, we can start the process of delivering a meaningful solution for them. Sometimes it only takes a moment to really understand where our user is coming from. Sometimes it takes several minutes of listening combined with empathetic statements such as "I understand why you feel that way." or "I'd feel that way, too, if I were in your situation." Regardless, until you can empathize with your user, you're not ready to start the technical aspects of the support session. Remember, it may be your technical expertise that solves the problem, but it's your skill in dealing with people that produces satisfied end-users.

As a support person, you convey empathy when you listen for the hidden meaning in what a user is saying, when you acknowledge the emotion, and when you offer caring assistance.

Empathy is especially important when dealing with a user who is irritated, angry or emotional. When users are emotional, it is difficult for them to act rationally. This is because of the way the human brain is structured. Our emotional brain, which is a relatively primitive part of the human brain, in essence "hijacks" the rest of our more rational, analytical brain and takes control.

To get someone out of the grip of the emotional brain and pass the power over to the analytical brain takes one of three things:

1. Intervention of a skilled listener or support professional

2. Effort on the part of the emotional person

3. The passage of time

It is important to understand this as we deal with emotional, upset or angry users. Empathy is a remedy for calming an emotional person by simply and genuinely acknowledging the emotion that the user feels. Empathy is very powerful because it diffuses emotion. If you want to be able to deal rationally with an emotional user, or if you simply want to ensure that an interaction does not escalate into an emotional one, remember to use empathy. When sincerely applied, empathy works like a charm in most situations.

Here are some examples of empathy statements:

- "I can hear how frustrated you are."

- "I can see how that would annoy you."

- "That's terrible!"

- "I understand how time-critical this is."

- "I would be unhappy if that happened to me, too."

Author and speaker Ross Shafer really gets to the heart of the matter when he points out that people don't really want customer service as much as they want customer empathy. The same concept applies to end-user support incidents. When you sincerely empathize with your user, you convey to them a sense of caring and understanding. There's a quote in customer service circles that says, "They don't care how much you know until they know how much you care." When a user believes that you genuinely care about their particular problem, no matter how many times you've heard it before, you're well on the way to creating a satisfied end-user before you even start to solve his or her problem!

Don R. Crawley is president and chief technologist at soundtraining.net, the Seattle training firm specializing in business skills training programs for IT professionals, plus accelerated technical training programs in the areas of Cisco and Linux products, plus workplace skills including customer service, project management, and time management. He works with IT professionals to enhance their work, lives, and careers.

Index

Onsite Training
Makes Sense!

*One- and two-day seminars
and workshops for I.T. professionals*

*Learning
solutions that
come right to
your door!*

soundtraining.net
accelerated i.t. training

Call (206) 988-5858 • soundtraining.net/onsite • Email: onsite@soundtraining.net